THE HORROR
BEHIND DOOR 213

Shortly before 11:30 P.M. on Monday, July 22, Tracy
Edwards dashed from a foul-smelling apartment, ran
left down 25th Street, and flagged down a patrolling
police car. Handcuffs dangled from one wrist as he
told the cops about a man who had held a knife to his
chest and threatened to cut out—and eat—his heart.
The cruiser raced around the block, and within mo-
ments, authorities had their first glimpse of the horror
behind door 213. The stench of rotting human flesh.
Eleven murder victims. Human heads in the freezer.
Torsos and body parts in a fifty-seven-gallon drum.
Vats of acid and preservatives. Polaroid pictures of
men in manacles, men being dismembered, men in
pieces . . .

WHO WAS THIS MAN? WHAT WAS IT IN HIS
PSYCHE THAT TRIGGERED SUCH A BLOODY
SERIAL KILLING SPREE? THE STARTLING AN-
SWERS ARE HERE, IN . . .

MILWAUKEE MASSACRE
Jeffrey Dahmer and the Milwaukee Murders

QUANTITY SALES

Most Dell books are available at special quantity discounts when purchased in bulk by corporations, organizations, or groups. Special imprints, messages, and excerpts can be produced to meet your needs. For more information, write to: Dell Publishing, 666 Fifth Avenue, New York, NY 10103. Attention: Director, Diversified Sales.

Please specify how you intend to use the books (e.g., promotion, resale, etc.)

INDIVIDUAL SALES

Are there any Dell books you want but cannot find in your local stores? If so, you can order them directly from us. You can get any Dell book currently in print. For a complete up-to-date listing of our books and information on how to order, write to: Dell Readers Service, Box DR, 666 Fifth Avenue, New York, NY 10103.

MILWAUKEE MASSACRE

Jeffrey Dahmer and the Milwaukee Murders

Robert J. Dvorchak and Lisa Holewa

A DELL BOOK

Published by
Dell Publishing
a division of
Bantam Doubleday Dell Publishing Group, Inc.
666 Fifth Avenue
New York, New York 10103

ISBN: 0-440-21286-3

Printed in the United States of America

Published simultaneously in Canada

October 1991

10 9 8 7 6 5 4 3 2 1

RAD

Contents

Preface

This has been a disturbing story to write in a number of ways. Likewise, it will be a disturbing story to read. The sheer magnitude of seventeen lives extinguished is bothersome enough. The pattern and particulars of how they died speaks to the dark potential of the human condition.

Jeffrey Lionel Dahmer began life ordinarily enough in Milwaukee and moved away as a boy. When he returned as a tormented young man, he made an indelible mark. In the custody of police, he said he killed seventeen times, in a manner that was as morbid as any murder anywhere. The oldest victim was thirty-three, the youngest, fourteen.

Nothing that follows is meant to be judgmental. It was the authors' intent to present the facts as best as they were known.

We make no claim at drawing conclusions. Work

has just begun by experts plumbing the depths of a mind troubled by emotional demons. It may be some time before answers are presented, and those answers will themselves be subject to interpretation and debate. More will be learned as the wheels of justice slowly grind away, and that work is just beginning. Perhaps only Dahmer himself will ever really know the answer.

All the victims were strangers to the man involved; he had no personal grudge against any of them. In some cases, there is nothing left to indicate what happened except the word of the man who said he did it. Parts of this puzzle are without pieces.

As to Dahmer himself, there are only snippets of information: revelations by an anguished family who knew him to be afflicted, recollections by childhood friends and army colleagues who sensed odd behavior, bewilderment by neighbors who had privately wondered what he was up to.

There are those who can argue—with plenty of justification—that this serial killer should have been stopped somewhere along the line of the thirteen years he operated. Where were the parents? Guidance counselors in school? The army? The police? The criminal justice system? The probation office? The neighbors? Is society so hardened it ignores signs of trouble? If all are to blame, are any to blame?

The urge to fix such blame is strong, as if pointing to one single culprit could explain such a calamity. But if the finger is pointed at one, can't it also be pointed back at others?

The clues and footprints, in fairness, seem much weightier in hindsight. No one knew of the cumulative picture until well after two cops investigating a complaint stumbled across a ghoulish discovery.

What is also disturbing is the absence of a heroic figure. Glenda Cleveland, a neighbor who had raised questions with police about Dahmer, believed her conscience when somebody else bought a lie. She squawked and prodded, but she couldn't convince anyone to pay attention until it was too late. Some police did their jobs, others are open to second-guessing. Some neighbors, so insulated from others' actions by the harsh prospect of their own daily survival, complained of strange odors in their building, but none griped loud enough to force someone to discover human carrion. A prosecutor sensed worrisome signals, but her argument went unheeded.

Families and communities are left wondering why. There is pain and anger and anguish and wrenching feelings to be sorted out and addressed before wounds can mend. It is likely to take a long time for the healing process to work.

At this writing, there is no light. There is no

rallying point around which to reaffirm that while something bad may have happened, something good stopped it before it spread. Perhaps that is the most disturbing thing of all.

1

Door of Evil

The door buzzer stirred John Batchelor just after his head hit the pillow. It was 11:25 P.M.

"Who is it?" Batchelor asked sleepily through the intercom.

"This is the police. Let us in."

Batchelor hit the button that opened the front door to the Oxford Apartments. He knew he hadn't done anything wrong and wondered what the hell was going on.

He peered out of his door to see Milwaukee police officers Robert Rauth and Rolf Mueller walking down the hallway accompanied by a black man who had handcuffs dangling from his left wrist.

The cops ignored Batchelor and rapped on the door marked 213. Their shift ended at midnight. With any luck, they could clear this up quickly and be on their way home.

A sandy-haired man wearing a blue T-shirt and dirty jeans peeped through the hole in the door, then quietly and coolly let them in. In the dying minutes of July 22, they had just entered the netherworld of Jeffrey Dahmer. A strange odor immediately tightened their stomachs and heightened their curiosity.

Rauth and Mueller came to this one-bedroom apartment after hearing a wild story told by Tracy Edwards. They were on patrol in their squad car when Edwards approached the driver's side and said he needed to rid himself of some handcuffs. The policemen wanted to know who put the steel bracelet on and why.

Edwards motioned in the direction of the Oxford Apartments, a low-rise building with a cream-colored facade in the middle of 25th Street. He told the police a man with a knife had threatened to cut out—and eat—his heart.

The cops radioed in, telling the shift supervisor in District Three that they were investigating a report of a possible assault on 25th Street between State and Kilbourn, a tough neighborhood on the city's west side. With Edwards in tow, they drove their squad car—a white Chevrolet Caprice with the

Milwaukee Police Department logo on the front doors—toward State Street and turned left. Without sirens or flashing lights, they stopped in front of 924 N. 25th Street.

The door to Dahmer's apartment was protected by an electronic security system, a high-tech gadget for a low-rent neighborhood. He told neighbors he needed it because he had been robbed.

Alarmed by the odor, Rauth and Mueller, with thirteen and ten years on the force respectively, walked with Edwards into a single space that formed the kitchen and living room. A sliding door to their right opened to the bathroom and bedroom.

A sofa was placed against the right wall. On the far side of the room, to the right of a window, was a four-foot-wide fish tank on a black table. A decorative animal horn hung above it. There were posters of bare-chested men and a magazine with a nude male on the cover. A lava lamp sat on a table, and there were two statues of griffins—a mythical animal with the body of a lion and the head of an eagle. On the kitchen stove were some pots and a gooey residue. It wasn't anything anybody wanted to touch. The sink was filled with dirty dishes.

As the cops checked out Edwards's story, the conversation spilled through the closed doorway into the hall. They wanted to know why Dahmer had threatened this guy.

"I just lost my job and I want to drink some fucking beer," Batchelor heard Dahmer reply.

Dahmer, thirty-one, had talked his way out of trouble before. Just two months earlier, three police officers had been at his apartment without suspecting anything was amiss. And that time he was in the company of a luckless Laotian boy whom neighbors had seen naked in the street.

One of the uniformed men reached for his portable radio—Handie-Talkies the cops call them—and asked headquarters to run Dahmer's name through the computer. It was basic police work. If a guy's making trouble, check if he's been in trouble before. The word came back: the guy had a felony conviction for second-degree sexual assault and enticing a thirteen-year-old boy. He was still on probation.

Through the closed door, residents heard Dahmer screech and scream. Batchelor heard someone yell what sounded like, "Faggot!"

"Ah, the son of a bitch just scratched me," Batchelor heard someone say.

There was more crashing and thumping.

"Oh God, he's going into one of those homo modes again," Batchelor heard a voice say.

When things settled, Batchelor heard one of the officers say, "All right, now what the hell is going on?"

This time, it was Tracy Edwards who spoke. He said he met Dahmer at the Grand Avenue Mall—a

downtown shopping district and meeting place—
then came back here for a beer.

"Next thing I knew, we was sitting down on the
couch and he was trying to put his arms around me.
When I refused, he went and got those cuffs. Then
he went to get the knife," Edwards said.

The cops escorted Edwards out into the hallway.
Through the open door, Batchelor saw Dahmer
lying facedown on the floor before one of the policemen told Batchelor: "Get the fuck back inside."

Batchelor said he overheard Edwards yelling: "I
got six kids. I love women. I ain't no fag."

All Edwards said he wanted to do was get back
to his brother's place on Wisconsin Avenue to avoid
any more of this mess. That's when one of the
officers must have opened Dahmer's refrigerator.

"Oh my God! There's a goddamn head in here.
He's one sick son of a bitch," Batchelor heard a
voice say.

Jeffrey Dahmer had been found out.

The ghoulish sight of the graying, waxen flesh
on Oliver Lacy's severed head made even a veteran
officer gag. Later, still shaken hours after his first
peek inside, Mueller said, "You think you've seen
it all here, and then something like this happens."

Batchelor bolted toward the phone and called
WISN-TV, Channel 12, and told them they might
want to get down there. Then a wail from Dahmer
pierced the air. All those forces seething inside him

erupted to life, transforming an outwardly quiet loner into a raving madman. "It was a screeching I'll never forget. It was terrible. It almost made me throw up," Batchelor recalled weeks later.

Inside, one of the cops kept Dahmer pinned to the floor. "Go get the shackles for the son of a bitch," Batchelor heard someone say.

The wheels of police work turned quickly now. The portable radio crackled to life again. The police alerted the lieutenant working as the shift supervisor at District Three headquarters, some twenty-five blocks away at 45th and Vliet. The lieutenant flashed the first sketchy but grisly details to homicide, and three detectives raced to the scene. The reinforcements arrived within minutes.

Then more police came. Neighbors saw uniformed men excitedly running up and down the steps, five and six at a time now. The apartment building had been invaded by badges.

After about twenty minutes, Dahmer was led out. He was shackled at the feet and wrists. As he shambled to a paddy wagon wearing the restraint, two policemen were in front of him and two behind.

"He looked weird, like a fucking geek that had gone nuts. He was like a maniac, like he was possessed," Batchelor said.

Randy Jones, who lives downstairs in No. 103, had heard a man—it turned out to be Tracy Edwards—screaming, bumping around, and running in the hallway shortly before 11:30. But people often come into the building drunk, so Jones went back to sleep.

Now, forty minutes later, the whole building seemed to be alive. Jones heard more thumps and shouts above him as police led Dahmer out. "He was hollering like an animal," Jones said.

After a quick appraisal that there were body parts inside the apartment, the first three homicide detectives on the scene called the medical examiner's office. Two forensic investigators arrived at 12:45 A.M. They began taking a clinical but grim inventory, noting the details in a report that became part of the police file.

Oliver Lacy's severed head was in a box on the bottom shelf of the refrigerator. It had been there a week. It sat next to an open box of Arm & Hammer baking soda, a kitchen staple struggling to absorb unwanted odors.

Inside the freezer compartment were three plastic bags. They turned out to be Oliver Lacy's heart, which Dahmer told police he saved "to eat later," and other human organs.

By 3 A.M., in a separate waist-high freezer, investigators determined that three plastic bags, fastened with twists, contained the heads of Matt Turner, Jeremiah Weinberger, and Joseph Bradehoft. They discovered biceps and other body parts, more hints that Dahmer had a taste for human flesh in addition to his taste for blood.

Now the district attorney's office was alerted.

More police cruisers converged on the scene, dome lights flashing, sirens wailing. Cruisers crowded the brick alley to the right of the Oxford. There must have been fifty cars there. It looked like half the Third District and the whole homicide squad was there. Lifeline paramedics were called; their services were long past being of help.

Startled residents, angry at missing sleep but accustomed to middle-of-the-night police calls, soon realized something extraordinary was happening to draw this much response. What they heard through their doors and walls confirmed their suspicions.

Police were heard shouting:

"Jesus Christ, he's got dead bodies around."

"This goddamn guy's crazy."

"There are hands and a head in the closet."

Inside, more details were noted. Dahmer's bedroom door had its own electronic security system, which locked on the outside. With this arrangement, someone could be confined inside.

Police found the knife that he had used to threaten Tracy Edwards, and a beer can, under the bed. Two human skulls were found on the top shelf of a closet, two more were in a computer box, and three others in the top drawer of a filing cabinet.

Three had been painted gray and looked like the plastic models used in science labs. In the bottom drawer of the same cabinet were an assortment of bones.

Against the wall near a window was a blue fifty-seven-barrel drum with a black lid. An overpowering smell assaulted the nose of the detective who opened it. Jammed inside were the headless torsos of Turner, Weinberger, and Bradehoft.

Decomposed hands and genitals were found in a metal kettle in the closet. There were vats of acid.

Pictures of nude men hung on the wall above Dahmer's bed and in his bathroom. Several pornographic videos and a tape of *The Exorcist* were scattered about the bedroom, where he kept his remote-controlled TV and VCR. He also had a personal computer, and on the bed was a Polaroid camera.

A photo diary and two skulls were found in the cardboard computer box. More pictures were found in the drawer of a bedroom dresser drawer and atop the freezer in the kitchen.

They showed "males in different degrees of surgical excision," in the clinical language of the report filed by forensic investigator Shirley Gaines. In plain words, they had been slaughtered. The photos showed men in various stages of undress, some wearing manacles like the ones Tracy Edwards had on.

One of those pictured was Konerak Sinthasom-phone. The only other remnant left of the fourteen-year-old boy was his fleshless skull. Nobody knew then how his death would haunt the police department and the city, until it came out that police who found the boy naked and dazed in the street allowed Dahmer to take him back into his apartment. And nobody knew at the time it was his brother who had been molested by Dahmer.

Police searching the apartment removed an electric saw, bottles of ethyl alcohol, chloroform, formaldehyde, a pickling liquid called muriatic acid, and a container of Lysol spray disinfectant.

They found ID cards for Bradehoft and Oliver Lacy. There were also prescription bottles for Lorazepam, a tranquilizer, and Doxepin, an antidepressant. These were written out to Dahmer by the state Department of Corrections.

The only foodstuffs found—outside of Lacy's heart and the biceps Dahmer later told police he fried in vegetable oil—were potato chips, beer, and a jar of mustard. Some fish food was also found on a table.

Nothing was skipped over. In the nuts-and-bolts of police work, anything may be a piece of evidence or a piece needed to put a puzzle together. The basics are the same at any crime scene, whether it's a burglary, a car wreck, or suspected serial murders. Dahmer had to be questioned and his story checked out. Dead men had to be identified and their families notified. Physical evidence had to be inventoried and processed. Investigators sought witnesses and people who knew Dahmer for any clues about what had happened. Crimes were easy to discover. Proving them in court within the restraints of the law was another matter.

In custody, police found Dahmer totally cooperative. It was as if the torment of thirteen years of harboring sinister secrets had been lifted from his soul.

He told a story the cops wrote down—Milwaukee police don't ordinarily use a tape recorder or video camera. It was a story that was hard to believe, one that was detailed in the criminal complaints filed by the district attorney.

According to statements taken by police, Dahmer said he killed seventeen people—all of them male, all of them strangers—beginning with a hitchhiker in Ohio just two weeks after he graduated from high school thirteen years earlier. Authorities found the remains of eleven males in his apartment.

Dahmer said he lured victims with promises of money if they posed for pictures, watched porn movies, or had sex. Then Dahmer said he put sleeping potions in their drinks, strangled them, and cut them up. He said he used the bathtub as a convenient chopping block; some body parts were flushed down the adjoining toilet, other flesh was dissolved in a fifty-seven-gallon drum of acid. He said he sometimes had sex with his victims before he killed them; on four occasions, sex happened after they were dead.

David Thomas died a peculiar death. Dahmer had decided he wasn't his type, but he said he killed Thomas anyhow. He figured the guy would be so angry at having been drugged that he might tip the cops. He disposed of the entire body. There wasn't a thing left, only Dahmer's word that the grisly event happened at all.

Along the way, Dahmer said he started keeping skulls as souvenirs or totems to keep him company in his solitude. He boiled them in kettles atop a stove, making a ghoulish pottage of removed flesh. One of the skulls was from a man who Dahmer admitted killing in his grandmother's home in the Milwaukee suburb of West Allis. Along with his former home in Ohio and the dingy apartment, it was the second of three killing grounds he used.

Back on 25th Street, police evacuated all the apartments on Dahmer's floor. Neighbors poured into the streets, some wearing nightclothes or whatever they could throw on. Nobody could sleep anyhow, what with the commotion.

Channel 12's van had arrived with the first camera crew. Beat reporters from the two Milwaukee newspapers, the *Journal* and the *Sentinel*, caught the chatter on the police scanners and headed for the scene. City newsrooms pulsed with life. Reporters worked the crowd for details. It wouldn't be long before the wire services and networks flashed the news around the globe. It was of particular interest in Germany, where Dahmer had spent time in the army and where there were some unsolved murders.

Curious neighbors from adjoining apartments swelled the ranks of the assembling throng to about three hundred. There were so many uniforms around, it looked like G-Day in Kuwait.

Dahmer had long before been taken away. Police had asked Channel 12 not to film when they brought him out of the apartment. "If that was a black guy they'd allow them to have that camera down his throat," someone yelled. It was the first hint of racial unrest in this predominantly black neighborhood. The Dahmer discovery was like lighting a fuse. The crimes were bad enough. Very soon, latent feelings in the community about police sensitivities would be going off.

Police in plainclothes carried down six boxes of evidence from upstairs. Cardboard boxes marked "skull" were placed in the medical examiner's white station wagon. The backseats were down to make room for the haul.

Through the window of the car, onlookers saw a skull that still had hair on it.

But something else was going on. Men wearing

yellow protective suits, breathing masks, hard hats, and heavy gloves lugged some large things down the steps.

A refrigerator was carried out and placed in a truck owned by TJ Contractors, a chemical company that specializes in hazardous cargo. People said they could smell the refrigerator blocks away.

An audible gasp went up when the men in chemical suits brought down the blue barrel. Their labored breathing could be heard through their air masks.

The ghastly discoveries quickly set neighbors abuzz over bothersome mysteries surrounding a loner who was one of the few whites living in the building. What were the putrid odors that had been dismissed as spoiled groceries or a backed-up toilet or the garbage Dumpster outside? Why were there sounds of an electric saw that everyone figured was being used to build something? What were thumps heard through the floorboards, initially shrugged off as men engaging in drunken horseplay? The reports of bodies in the apartment made imaginations sizzle.

The Oxford Apartments building, a rectangular low-rise brick structure of forty-nine units, was built in 1962. Owned by Metropolitan Associates, it offers government-subsidized housing for those with low incomes. It was no stranger to crime. On May 4, 1991, a resident was murdered on the third floor.

Police said Dean M. Vaughn, twenty-six, was strangled to death with someone's bare hands. The crime had not been solved at the time of Dahmer's arrest.

Two blocks from the apartment building stand two strip joints where men come to drink beer and ogle bare-breasted dancers. Hookers solicit business on nearby State Street. Street gangs oversee daylight drug deals. Kids play in lots littered with garbage and discarded car parts. Apartments and storefronts are boarded up.

Tree-lined 25th Street does not look as ferocious as the war zones in Harlem, the Bronx, north Philadelphia, East Los Angeles, or East St. Louis. But it is getting more down-at-the-heels, and residents were resignedly getting used to its woes.

In the past ten years, the neighborhood had changed from 37 percent black to 69 percent black. The percentage of whites had dropped from 54 percent to 18 percent since 1980, according to census figures.

Almost 90 percent of the neighborhood residents are renters, most of them in multiunit buildings, and the median rent is $280, well below the Milwaukee and Wisconsin average. Dahmer paid $296 a month for his one-bedroom place.

Median home value is $33,000, about half of what homes are valued for in the city as a whole.

Now people were staring at the Oxford Apartments building as if it were Dracula's castle or a real-life house of horrors.

In the apartment directly below Dahmer's, Aaron Whitehead was telling reporters he was often roused from his sleep by loud pounding and scuffling. "One night, I heard what sounded like a kid up there. He was crying like his mother had just walloped him. Then I heard a big falling sound, like he was being hurt."

Another time, the thumping and crashing got so loud that Whitehead rushed to a corner of his bedroom. "I got out of my bed because I thought they would come right through the ceiling," he said. He didn't report the incident, which quieted down after about ten minutes.

Things that went thump in the night weren't the only sounds.

"I would hear a buzz saw running in the early evening. I thought he was building something," said Pamela Bass, who lived across the hall from Dahmer in No. 214.

"I used to hear him over there talking to himself, cussing to himself, talking real loud, and I knew he didn't have anyone over there."

Then there was the smell, the pervasive stench of rotting human flesh. Nobody who's ever inhaled the odors from a decomposing body ever forgets the way the smell crinkles the nose. But nobody expected the smell of death to be coming from a one-bedroom apartment.

"We've been smelling things for weeks, but we thought it was a dead animal, or something like that. We had no idea it was humans," said Ella Vickers, a neighbor.

Some checked behind ovens and refrigerators for dead rodents. Some gave up looking for the source and burned incense to mask the stench.

John Batchelor, in one of the few meetings he ever had with Dahmer, asked him to do something about the odor.

"I got tired of coming home and smelling that shit. Sometimes you could smell it all the way down on the first floor," Batchelor said. When he invited guests over to visit, he instructed them to hold their noses until they passed Dahmer's door.

Larry Marion, who was the building manager when Dahmer moved into No. 213 in May of 1990, said the smell was so bad in the spring that residents complained. "Had we been veterans, we would have known the stench of death," he told reporters.

When confronted, Dahmer always seemed to smooth-talk his way out of it. He blamed spoiled meat or a balky fish tank, always promising obligingly to fix it so that he wouldn't be a bother to anyone. Several times, apartment managers told him to clean up his freezer. Generally the smell would die down, so they wouldn't report it to authorities. Then it would start all over again. It got especially bad in the hot weather.

"He told me the smell was from his freezer— rotten meat. I believed him. I had no reason not to believe him," said Pamela Bass. She slipped a note about the problem under Dahmer's door, and confronted him several times.

She and her husband, Vernell, allowed WLS, an all-talk radio station from Chicago, to broadcast its morning show from their apartment two days after the discovery. The question that callers asked most frequently was, "How does it smell?"

Nanetta Lowery, twenty-one, lived above Dahmer in No. 313. She bitched so much that management granted her demands to move to a new unit, but no one went below to check the source in Dahmer's place.

"The smell got so bad, it got in my clothes and I couldn't get it out, even after washing. How were we supposed to know it was dead people?" Lowery told reporters.

"My father said it smelled like death. But I just joked it off. You'd never imagine that it would turn out to be what it was," Lowery said.

The smell was noticeable even on an adjoining property. Gene Mitchell got whiffs of it from his place. "I thought it was sewage. You'd just open the door and you'd smell it."

The neighborhood, just blocks from Marquette University, was hardened by random violence and callused by what residents perceived as neglect. Jeffrey Dahmer was a testament to how much faith people had lost in the system. The basic law of survival here was simply to mind your own business.

Besides, who expects your neighbor to be killing and mutilating people and saving the remains? People tend to see what they want to see.

Pat Laur, who lives at the corner of 24th Street and Kilbourn, said gunshots and strange noises were so commonplace, she didn't bother to call police anymore.

"It used to be, if we heard a scream at night we were all ears," Laur said. "Now if we hear a scream, we really don't hear it."

John Batchelor saw police scouring Dahmer's apartment, checking out the Polaroids. "This one's got his chest cut open and he's pouring acid down it," he heard one cop say.

Police Chief Philip Arreola, just eighteen months on the job as the city's top cop, came to inspect the scene in the morning. He held the first of what would be dozens of news conferences and media events outside the Oxford Apartments.

At a later news conference, Medical Examiner Jeffrey Jentzen said the remains found in the apartment were "not inconsistent with cannibalism. . . . We may have opinions on that at a future time."

A police padlock went up on No. 213, along with a sign that said EVIDENCE in pink letters.

Soon neighborhood kids would come in just to touch the door. Some would tiptoe down the hallway to sniff it. A morbid fascination would flourish. People would come from all over the city to look at the building, ignoring the traffic barriers police set up at both ends of the block.

The next day, residents said people fired random gunshots at the building and threatened to blow the place up. The residents were being blamed for not noticing something sooner.

A month after the discovery only three units were occupied.

The Oxford Apartments would never be the same. Neither would the neighborhood, nor the city.

On the night of the grisly discoveries, Tracy Edwards stood outside with the crowd, watching the police carrying out barrels and containers filled with human heads and body parts. The truth spilled out of that apartment with every gruesome item.

At first, Edwards knew he had survived a close call. Then he realized he had escaped a human torture chamber and butcher shop. He considered himself extremely lucky for having outsmarted and outmuscled a captor whose bloodlust had been un-slaked for thirteen years.

Seventeen others before him didn't make it. One was a hitchhiker, another a runaway. Two were fourteen-year-old boys, hardly past puberty. Others were casual homosexual contacts lured from gay bars, street corners, or bus stops. Some were free spirits and risk-takers, vulnerable to a come-on by a sharp-featured white man. Some were aspiring models who loved to have their picture taken, especially if someone was willing to give them money to do it. The oldest one was thirty-three.

Almost all of them had known Dahmer for only a few hours. Yet they willingly ventured inside a stranger's foul-smelling apartment.

Eleven were black, one Laotian, one Hispanic, one Native American, three white.

They had one thing in common: they were available. And the way they lived their lives made many of them hard to trace if they turned up missing.

Tracy Edwards, thirty-two, said he has fathered six children by as many women. But he was out looking to party on July 22 when he ran into Dahmer at the Grand Avenue Mall.

Edwards, a laborer and a roofer, moved from Tupelo, Mississippi, in June to live with a brother, Jerome, who lives near Dahmer's neighborhood. Another brother, Terry, and his father also live in Milwaukee.

Edwards had seen Dahmer around, and the two struck up a conversation at Milwaukee's Grand

Avenue Mall. They made plans to meet some other people for an impromptu party, but first took a cab to the apartment where Edwards's brother lived. No one was home, so Edwards accepted Dahmer's invitation to come back to his apartment. They stopped for two six-packs of Budweiser along the way.

The streetwise Edwards said Dahmer appeared to be an ordinary guy. "He seemed like a normal person. If I had any self-doubt, I wouldn't have gone," he said.

Indeed, the professionals who profile serial killers marvel at how well they can blend in, at how they can appear to be so average, at how well they can gain someone's trust before their monstrous psyche surfaces.

For example, Ted Bundy was executed in 1989 after admitting he killed twenty-eight women. Up until the time Florida threw the switch with him in an electric chair called "Old Sparky," Bundy was receiving marriage proposals from women captivated by his looks and charms.

And John Wayne Gacy is on death row in Illinois for torturing and killing thirty-three boys and young men, then burying most in the crawl space under his house. Gacy is known as the "Clown Killer"; he often dressed in clown's costumes and cheery makeup as a hobby.

Dahmer could never have operated for so long if

he came across as a raving lunatic or behaved like a fire-breathing creature from the black lagoon. He stands six feet tall, weighs 185 pounds, and is of medium build, with sandy hair and brown eyes.

Dahmer's nonthreatening charm may have gotten Edwards inside his apartment, but he had to do some fast talking to explain the stench. Dahmer apologized—"He said it was sewage," Edwards said. Because he planned to stay for only one beer, Edwards came in despite the bizarre odor. How many others had noticed the stench, but disregarded it to enter the apartment is a secret known only to the dead.

A nightmare was about to begin, or as Edwards called it, "a four-hour period of hell."

Edwards sipped a drink, then felt a little woozy as if something had been slipped into it. He wanted to leave.

But when Edwards, 5-foot-11 and a wiry 160 pounds, started getting restless, Dahmer changed radically. The hollow eyes flashed widely. His nondescript face was now flushed with power. His voice became icy and commanding.

Edwards was sitting on the sofa, watching the fish swim in the tank to his right, when Dahmer pulled handcuffs and a knife seemingly from nowhere. It was a practiced motion, something Dahmer had perfected on other guests.

While he was holding a beer can in his right

hand, Edwards felt steel lock around his left wrist. His chest felt the point of a knife blade.

Dahmer's voice sounded as if it came from the bottom of a tomb. He had control now.

"He went from Mr. Right to Mr. It. It was as if I was confronting Satan himself," Edwards said. "He said he was going to cut my heart out and eat it."

But first, Dahmer wanted his guest to strip and pose for pictures. It was part of his routine: giving orders, fulfilling fantasies, making men do what he wanted them to do.

Edwards stalled for time, playing along by unbuttoning his shirt and sitting on the couch to drink more beers while trying to talk his way out of this mess. He'd been in tough spots before and he needed to think.

Lord, how am I going to get out of here? Edwards thought.

Dahmer ordered Edwards to the bedroom at knifepoint, but Edwards was able to talk his way back to the living room.

Edwards appealed to Dahmer as a friend not to hurt him. He considered jumping from a window. During several trips to the bathroom to relieve himself of the Budweiser, he studied Dahmer's door locks to figure out how quickly he could flee.

Finally, when the clock moved past 11 P.M., Edwards made his move.

"Either he's going to have to kill me, or I'm going to have to kill him," Edwards thought.

Edwards delivered a karate punch to Dahmer's face, then rocketed for the door. Before he could get through the doorway, Dahmer caught him by the wrists and offered to remove the handcuffs if Edwards would come back inside.

Edwards wriggled free and shot down the hall. He sprinted from the apartment building and turned left on 25th Street, where Earl Peterson saw the handcuffed man running toward Kilbourn Street.

"He was hollering 'Help!' He flagged down an officer and brought him back to the building," Peterson said.

Later, after watching police discover the horrors Dahmer had committed previously to less fortunate houseguests, Edwards breathed a huge sigh of relief.

"I feel I'm grateful to be alive," he said. "If I hadn't gotten away, this guy might still be operating. It's like God sent me in there to get this guy."

He also sounded like a penitent child, one who after the fact remembers those parental admonitions about not going home with strangers.

"I don't want any new friends anymore," he said. "I'm happy with who I know and who I'm friends with now. I don't want to meet any new people."

Three weeks later, Edwards's luck soured. A

grand jury in Lee County, Mississippi, had indicted Edwards in November 1990 on a charge of sexual battery involving a fourteen-year-old girl, but he was not arrested or formally arraigned. Edwards thought, and according to news accounts, records indicated that the case had been dismissed when the girl failed to show at a hearing.

Mississippi authorities didn't know where Edwards was until they heard about his exploits in Milwaukee, and they asked the police to hold him on a fugitive warrant pending an extradition hearing. He was later released on bail.

"It came to our attention this was the same person for whom we had an indictment for sexual battery," said Lee County assistant district attorney Rob Coleman.

2

Mystery Man

The mystery behind the Milwaukee massacre starts with a simple question. Who is Jeffrey L. Dahmer?

Trying to answer it, however, only seems to deepen the mystery. How did he operate for so long without getting caught? Why did he kill? What inner torment drove him? How could *anybody* do what he is accused of? Why was he coming clean to authorities now? Could he be believed?

Police Chief Philip Arreola announced at his first news conference that investigators would look into deeper themes after Dahmer gave his statements to police.

''We're not investigating a who-done-it. We're

investigating why it was done and how it was done,"
Arreola said.

Experts who study the inner workings of the
mind may spend years trying to clear things up, and
no one may ever know how a man who worked and
mingled among the masses could script his own
real-life *Silence of the Lambs* and do things that
might startle the fictional Hannibal the Cannibal.

He was a loner who feared abandonment. As a
child, he kept animal skulls and bones; as an adult,
the keepsakes were human parts. He planted flowers for his grandmother, but admitted to killing and
butchering men in her basement. If authorities
couldn't stop him, why didn't he have the guilt, the
remorse, the revulsion to stop himself?

There are no easy explanations to the machina-
tions of a monstrous heart, one so tortured it vainly
sought to fill up its emptiness with booze, and by
the horror of sex with dead men. There are clues to
a burgeoning evil. In retrospect, they seem far
weightier than at the time they were first observed.

Dahmer cried out for attention, even if subcon-
sciously, from an early age. But those cries weren't
heard. Not by parents too absorbed in their own
personal wars during a bitter divorce that left their
son feeling abandoned. Not by puzzled classmates,
and top brass when Dahmer served in the Army.
Not by a judge who gave him probation instead of a

jail sentence for molesting a boy. Not by an over-worked probation officer.

Dahmer, the older of two sons from a broken marriage, grew up in the well-to-do suburbs of Akron, Ohio. He moved to Milwaukee in 1982, living at first with his grandmother in suburban West Allis before renting his own apartment in the city.

A week before his arrest, Dahmer lost his job. It wasn't the first time he was a loser. He dropped out of Ohio State University in 1978 after one term; he got an early discharge from the army in 1981 because of heavy drinking.

Until he was fired on July 15 for chronic absenteeism, Dahmer worked for six and a half years on the graveyard shift at the Ambrosia Chocolate Co. As a laborer, he earned $8.25 an hour.

One of 380 employees, he worked as a mixer in the manufacturing department of a ninety-seven-year-old company that produced sweet brown confections that other candy-makers turned into candy bars. The sensuous smell of cocoa that wafted from the chocolate factory contrasted sharply with the rot in his apartment.

To his coworkers, Dahmer was aloof and friendless. He didn't volunteer much about his personal life, and nobody really inquired. Workers remember him dragging home discarded barrels to keep things in. He often walked home or rode the bus. He had no car. A cab driver remembers Dahmer taking the fifty-seven-gallon blue barrel back to the apartment in his taxi.

Dahmer kept his job while serving time for sexually molesting a thirteen-year-old Laotian boy. In January of 1989, he was convicted of second-degree sexual assault and enticing a child for immoral purposes. What he did was lure the boy to his apartment with a promise of $50 if he posed for pictures. According to the criminal complaint, Dahmer slipped a sleeping pill into the boy's coffee cup, then fondled him when he stood partially disrobed in front of the lens. It was the same way he treated other men, but somehow this boy got away. Dahmer's family believes the incident occurred the day Dahmer moved into his own apartment.

The convictions earned him prison terms of five years and three years, to be served concurrently, but the judge stayed the sentence. Instead, Dahmer was given a year under a work-release program at the Community Correctional Center, which allowed him to work in the chocolate factory at night and serve his time in a minimum security dormitory he shared with eighty to ninety men. Even at that, he only served ten months because of an early release.

No one knew it at the time, but he would later admit to having killed five times before his sentence. He resumed his grisly spree shortly after he was released on probation in March of 1990.

After the revelations of July 22, Dahmer's first

public pronouncement, delivered through his defense attorney, Gerald P. Boyle, was a desire to come clean.

"This is my fault. There is a time to be honest, and I want to be honest," Boyle quoted Dahmer as saying.

Boyle said of his client, "He just wanted to end it. He just wanted to give the police a full and complete statement of his involvement. He said he had no one to blame but himself. Not the system, not the courts, not the probation officer."

Boyle had defended Dahmer during the child molestation case—an incident that gave the first hint of the torment within Dahmer.

"This is a very sick young man who has many kinds of mental problems," Boyle said after Dahmer's much darker crimes were discovered.

Dahmer's father, Lionel, a chemist with PPG Industries in Pittsburgh, spoke painfully of his son in select interviews with newspapers. "There's no doubt he's insane," Lionel Dahmer told the *Milwaukee Sentinel* just after the July 22 discoveries. "Jeff's never been socially adaptive. He's always been out of the social mainstream. I don't know how to put it. . . . Different."

Lionel went to Milwaukee after the arrest to see his son and look after his ailing mother, Catherine Dahmer, eighty-seven, who Jeffrey had lived with for a time and in whose house he had committed three murders. A retired school teacher, Catherine was recently ill with pneumonia. While there, Lionel was watching a Milwaukee television talk show on victims' rights and called in.

"I did not realize just how sick he was. I realize now that he is mentally ill, but I did not know the extent," he told Joe Smith, host of *Smith & Company*.

Asked what he would say to his son, Lionel Dahmer said, "I will say that I love him. And I will, as I always have, stand by him in my thoughts and prayers. I'm very grieved."

Shortly thereafter, he spoke to the *Akron Beacon Journal* about his son.

"How could anyone be polite and kind and pretty normal otherwise and yet do these horrible things, unless they are extremely troubled and insane?" said the fifty-five-year-old Dahmer. "He was a person who was basically kind but deeply, deeply troubled by something, and he has been for a long time."

Dahmer's stepmother, Shari, witnessed a life that had been in tatters and now seemed to be totally out of control.

"He couldn't embrace. He couldn't touch. His eyes were dead," she told *The Plain Dealer* of Cleveland. "This child has no heart left within him. He was a walking zombie."

Dahmer's mother, Joyce Flint, has shunned the

media, and disconnected her phone two days after the discoveries. She is a case manager for the Central Valley AIDS Team in Fresno, California, which provides counseling and other help to AIDS victims.

"Mrs. Flint doesn't have anything to say to anybody," said Patience Milrod, the woman's attorney. "You can imagine her state of mind. I think that she just feels that this is a time for her to deal privately with the trauma of these charges being brought. The only thing she has to say to anybody is that she loves her son and she just wants to be left alone."

Her son told his probation officer he had not heard from his mother for five years until she called him in March 1991. Between then and the time he was arrested, Dahmer said he killed eight times.

Joyce Flint, of Chippewa Falls, Wisconsin, married Lionel Dahmer, a chemistry student at Marquette University in Milwaukee, on August 22, 1959, in West Allis. Ten months later, on May 21, 1960, Jeffrey Dahmer was born at Evangelical Deaconess Hospital in Milwaukee.

It would be a troubled family.

Lionel earned a bachelor's degree in 1961 and a master's degree in 1962 from Marquette, then left with his family to get his doctorate in chemistry from Iowa State University.

In 1966, the family moved to northeastern Ohio to the suburbs west of Akron and south of Cleveland. This is where Jeffrey spent his formative years, where he developed his taste for alcohol, where he saw his parents battle, where he got his first chemistry set and tested it on animal flesh, where in his senior year in high school he went to the prom, got his degree, and he says, killed his first man.

When Lionel got a job in 1966 with PPG Industries in Barberton, it was a big year for young Dahmer. He moved into a new home, entered first grade at Hazel Harvey Elementary School, and got a baby brother, David, born December 18. There are hints—but no firm statements from family or friends—that Joyce Dahmer's second pregnancy was a difficult one. A teacher noted on a first grade report card that, during his mother's illness, six-year-old Jeffrey Dahmer felt "neglected." An ominous seed had been planted.

He didn't complete first grade at Hazel Harvey. The family moved and he enrolled in another school with a month left before summer vacation. A year later, the family moved again, this time to a ranch-style home on a 1.7-acre plot in Bath Township, a well-to-do suburb where the progeny of the Firestones and other powerbrokers from the nearby tire factories in Akron lived and frolicked.

The Dahmer home had a spring-fed pond and

plenty of neat things for kids at play: a crawl space that was perfect for creating a boy's own little world, a wooden shed up on the hill that made a great clubhouse. The estate was located at 4480 Bath Road, a country lane without sidewalks. It was an area of garden clubs and pampered tennis courts. Lionel Dahmer had played tennis in college; his son also took up the sport. The spacious lots, leafy shrubs, and manicured lawns were a far cry from the tough Milwaukee neighborhood of Jeffrey's later years, a neighborhood where drug dealers, prostitutes, and gangs prowled.

Something may have happened to Jeffrey Dahmer in his childhood that would help explain some things in his development. But like other episodes in Dahmer's life, it is murky.

A notation in Dahmer's probation file refers to an April 27, 1990, telephone conversation with Lionel Dahmer, who said when Jeffrey was eight he was abused by an eight-year-old neighbor boy. The parole officer's handwritten reference said Lionel wondered if the episode "may be reason why subject has problems with sexuality issues."

Jeffrey Dahmer, in his jail cell, told police he has no recollection of anything like that.

"We specifically asked the Milwaukee Police Department to ask Mr. Dahmer if he had either been sexually or physically abused as a child," said

Captain John Gardner of the Bath Township Police. "His answer was, 'No, not by anyone.' "

But this troubled childhood had plenty of pain, chief among them the bitter breakup of his parents' marriage and the disintegration of his home.

It was common knowledge that the Dahmers fought. That's one reason why few childhood chums ventured over to his house to play. Why endure two adults who always seemed to be at each other's throats?

Young Dahmer, caught in the middle of a messy battle, suffered in silence.

In 1977, Lionel Dahmer sued his wife of eighteen years for divorce. The divorce petition filed in Summit County courts charged his wife with "extreme cruelty and gross neglect of duty." She filed a countersuit, making similar charges.

The marriage officially was dissolved on July 24, 1978. Summit County Judge Richard V. Zurz ruled in favor of Mrs. Dahmer, concluding "unfortunate differences have arisen between the parties, making it impossible for them to live together any longer as husband and wife."

As part of the settlement, Joyce Flint was awarded $400 a month in alimony, $225 a month in child support, and custody of their son David. Jeffrey was eighteen, considered an adult by the court, and was excluded from the divorce arguments. Lionel Dahmer agreed to buy out her share of the home.

Before he moved out to a hotel, Lionel had retreated to a corner of the house, so he would have less contact with his spouse. An acquaintance said Dahmer even drew up a boundary with a primitive security system—a set of keys tied to a string that would jangle if his wife invaded his space.

During this protracted domestic war, and unbeknownst to Lionel, Mrs. Dahmer also moved out and took her younger son with her. Jeffrey, who as an adult was not part of the divorce proceedings, was left in an empty house with no money, no food, and a balky refrigerator.

Court documents reflect the raw emotions of the breakup. Lionel Dahmer sought custody of his younger son. His attorney, George A. Clark, argued against letting the boy go with his mother because of her "extensive mental illness." She got custody anyway, at least for a time. In 1982, the court would approve David's decision to go back and live with his father.

It was a two-sided battle. Mrs. Dahmer won a restraining order in court prohibiting the father from "molesting or assaulting or in any way disturbing her or the minor children," according to court documents quoted by the press.

In August, Mrs. Dahmer moved back to Chippewa Falls, Wisconsin, with her younger child. According to a complaint filed with the court by her ex-husband, she picked up, "leaving the older child, Jeffrey, alone in the house and having instructed him not to tell of the move."

The bickering outlived the marriage.

On August 6, 1980, two full years after the divorce, Mrs. Dahmer called Bath Township police to report a shouting and shoving match with her ex-husband. No charges were filed, and the police report noted, "Both parties advised they would be peaceful the remainder of the night." It was not clear why they were together at their former house, which Lionel was in the process of selling.

But neighbors said it wasn't the first time authorities had to be called to restore peace there.

"The police were out several times," said Susan Lehr, a former neighbor.

Lehr's four sons were once playmates of young Dahmer's. When they went on vacation, Jeffrey took over their paper route. And she, for one, noticed the domestic turbulence had disturbed the boy.

"At the time I knew him, there was something devastating going on in his life and there wasn't anybody there to help him. I feel bad about that," she said. "The potential for good was wasted. These are inhuman acts, yet a human being committed them. Why?"

The people who knew an adolescent Jeffrey

Dahmer may not have gauged the depth of his torment, but they did notice bizarre behavior and quirky pastimes.

On the Dahmer property, up on a hill away from the house and the garage, was a wooden shed that once housed yard tools and assorted instruments home owners collect.

For Jeffrey, it was a private castle. If his world was disrupted by fighting parents, he could shut it out and find solace in this wooden shack. Presently, it housed his most cherished childhood possessions.

He collected insects. He scoured the grounds and woods for specimens: praying mantises, butterflies, moths, spiders, dragonflies from the pond, bugs of all sorts. He locked them inside empty pickle jars, preserving them in formaldehyde. He arranged the glass exhibits on the shelves, and he found he had the power to make something last, something that wouldn't crumble on the whim of an argument.

The bugs worked out so well that he graduated to small animals: chipmunks and squirrels that lived in the trees behind his house; dogs and cats killed by the cars rolling down the country lane in front of his driveway; raccoons, groundhogs, opossums, rabbits, and small birds. Young Dahmer kept experimenting with more trophies.

Rotting flesh and disgusting smells were unpleasant side effects, but Dahmer learned that chemicals and acids could dissolve hides and skins, melt flesh, and leave bleached bones.

He even created an animal cemetery outside the shed. He buried the bodies, but impaled the skulls of chipmunks and squirrels on crosses.

"I remember that graveyard. He had quite a collection of skeletons," said Eric Tyson, a playmate who was three years younger than Dahmer.

Other boys collected baseball cards and childhood playthings. Dahmer would startle them by asking, "Want to go out and collect road kills?" He took his bike on the quiet country lanes and looked for dead things.

Tyson and a pal remember the day Dahmer showed them a large jar filled with a murky black liquid. Dahmer said it contained a raccoon, but the boys scoffed at him.

To prove he wasn't lying, Dahmer smashed the container on a rock, revealing the decomposing booty inside. The smell almost knocked everybody over.

Back then there were tales of pet dogs and cats that were killed and impaled on trees and stakes. But it wasn't until Dahmer was arrested that Jim Klippel called Bath Township police with an old memory. Klippel, a former neighbor, said that in 1975 he and a girlfriend found a dog's skull impaled on a stick; its body, skinned and gutted, was nailed to a nearby tree. The site was in the woods, about three hundred yards from the Dahmer home. He made another scary discovery about one hundred yards away. It was a fire pit ringed by thirteen smaller ones, something that looked like an occult sacrifice area.

"It was a pretty gruesome picture. It looked like some kind of devil worshiping to us," Klippel said.

No one is sure if this was Dahmer's handiwork, but Klippel recalled, "I heard stories about him going around and doing things to animals."

Other buddies remember going to a fishing hole near Bath and Medina roads. Most of the kids tossed back the bluegills and bass they hooked. Jeffrey Dahmer was different.

He took his catch and cut it up into tiny pieces with his pocket knife. Then he'd toss the minced remains back into the water, where other fish would rise to feed on them.

"Why do you cut them like that, Jeff?" one of the kids asked.

"I want to see what it looks like inside, I like to see how things work," Dahmer told him.

One playmate remembered another particular fascination of Dahmer's. He liked to listen to heartbeats, placing his hand or his ear against someone's chest to hear the buh-bump of life coursing through arteries and veins.

Years later, Dahmer was still feeling pulses. Except, these were the dying heartbeats of men being strangled. In his statements to police, Dahmer said he killed his victims by squeezing the life from them with his bare hands, a leather strap, or a barbell.

According to experts, strangulation is a favored method among serial killers.

3

Tormented Jester

School chums didn't think of Jeffrey Dahmer with clinical curiosity, wondering what made him tick. But to them, he drank too much and behaved too oddly not to attract attention.

Dahmer's relationship with the bottle was first noticed in seventh grade. Classmate Chip Crofoot noticed his stash of gin in his locker.

"I don't remember much about him other than his drinking. He pretty much kept to himself all the time," Crofoot recalled.

High school classmates said they smelled Scotch on his breath and noticed the beer cans ingeniously tucked inside the torn lining of an olive-drab army field jacket. That way he didn't have to go to his locker or leave the building for more alcohol.

In the habit's early stages, alcohol lowered Dahmer's inhibitions enough so he'd pull crazy antics: bleating like a sheep; faking epileptic fits; sitting in the quiet library and yelling out "Mrs. Shepherd," but never getting caught by the aging librarian.

At Revere High School, in a middle- to upper-class suburb dotted with shopping malls and winding roads, Dahmer referred to alcohol as his "medicine"—a self-prescribed tonic to dull some stab of pain. Booze fueled a penchant for wackiness, such as drawing chalk outlines of fictional bodies on the ground or pressing his nose up against the glass window of a door to make the kids laugh in German class.

Zany behavior had a distinctive panache: any screwy act became known as "doing a Dahmer." An astute psychiatrist may have been able to detect a troubled teen acting out some inner rage, but nobody at school noticed enough to confront him.

The only thing average about Dahmer's intelligence was the final grade. He made his share of As, dragged down by an equal share of Fs. He could excel and fail in the same subject, depending on the demons of his psyche.

The bespectacled Dahmer played clarinet and intramural tennis. He liked reading fiction, such as *Lord of the Rings*, and expressed an interest in chess and computers. As a senior, he started lifting weights with a new set of barbells. In his spare time, he waited tables at the pricey Lanning's Restaurant.

But Dahmer made his most memorable impression by being blanked out of a high school group picture where he didn't belong.

On page ninety-eight of the Revere senior yearbook are forty-five beaming members of the National Honor Society, the flower of the student body. But one senior three rows from the top has no face at all. There's just a spooky silhouette, blacked out with a marking pen, of Jeffrey Dahmer in his army jacket. In one of his trademark pranks, he had sneaked into the group portrait, where he certainly hadn't earned a spot. The president of the group was so incensed that he ordered Dahmer's image blotted out.

It became something of a cheap metaphor for Dahmer's life. He tried to get attention, but wound up being erased.

"Even at the time we thought it was creepy," said classmate Michael Kukral. "We said, 'Look, they killed Jeff. They cut off his head.' Everybody in school knew who it was."

It wasn't the only time Dahmer outsmarted the academics by sneaking into the honor society picture. He pulled the same stunt as a junior.

But there's another image that's just as haunting. Dahmer had his picture taken with the staff of

the *Lantern,* the school newspaper. Twelve colleagues are facing the camera. Dahmer, smack in
the middle of the group, is facing right. It looks like
a mug shot police take of a suspect's profile.

Dahmer proved he could be creative on a class
field trip to Washington, D.C. He called the White
House and talked his way into receiving an on-the-
spot tour of Vice President Walter Mondale's office.

He pulled another notable stunt for a group
called the Dahmer Fan Club. A half-dozen students
antcd up some pocket money, a total of $15 tu $20,
to watch Dahmer perform at the Summit County
Mall. He wanted the money to buy beer, and his
buddies supplied him with a six-pack for his command performance.

With the group watching but staying well out of
sight of security guards, Dahmer raced up the esca-
lators the wrong way, shouting "Out of my way!
Out of my way!"

Amid shoppers he faked having an epileptic fit,
then got up and walked away.

He'd go into stores and knock things over. He
spilled drinks at a lunch counter by poking them
with his umbrella. In front of the General Nutrition
Center, where a woman was handing out free sam-
ples, Dahmer loaded up his mouth with alfalfa
sprouts and sunflower seeds. Then he spit them at
the woman, yelling, "I'm allergic! I'm allergic! I'm

going to die." It looked a little like the food fight in *Animal House*.

Mike Kukral watched those juvenile pranks and laughed. Thirteen years later, he was reading a newspaper on a train in Czechoslovakia when he discovered the class jester had admitted to killing and butchering seventeen people. His blood curdled.

"By his senior year, he did have a drinking problem. He'd crack us all up with the things he did, but it wasn't the type of thing that hurt anybody. I didn't see him as a monster, but these acts he did were monstrous. It's like something slipped in his mind one day and he became a different person. We knew he was a little different, but none of us suspected this. None of us can figure out what put him over the edge," Kukral said.

Dahmer learned he could fall through the cracks. Students thought he was the responsibility of teachers, who thought he should be disciplined by guidance counselors, who thought he should be handled by the police, who passed him on to the judges.

"His behavior manifested a deep need for some sort of attention," said classmate Jim Gibbs, a writer living in Washington. "He was desperate for attention. But he wasn't considered anybody's responsibility. No one ever confronted him or tried to help him. No one ever did anything about it. We just found ways to ignore him."

Dahmer didn't talk much in school, but everyone knew his parents' marriage was dying. Something inside Dahmer's heart seemed to be dying too.

"There were a lot of problems at home. We all heard about his parents arguing and fighting. It wasn't a place to go over and visit," Mike Kukral said. "He used to have that little grin. From what I've seen, that grin is gone."

There was one more ritual to complete.

Jeffrey Dahmer, who didn't go to parties and didn't date, went to the prom with Bridget Geiger, two years his junior and the friend of a friend. She had long hair and wore a long, powder-blue gown; he didn't wear a tuxedo or a jacket, opting for a dark-brown vest and a big bow tie. She remembered he was so nervous he couldn't pin on the corsage, so her mother did it for him.

Dahmer, painfully shy, never danced with his date. He even left her sitting at a table while he went to McDonald's for some cheeseburgers. She saw the wrappers in his car.

"It was bad enough that I got coaxed into this, then he left me sitting there," said Geiger, now married and the mother of two. "He didn't say two words to me. He didn't even kiss me good-night. He shook my hand."

Within the next few weeks, Dahmer invited her to a party at his house. She called it a "nerd" scene, with about five people there. There was no food and no music, but there was a séance and one of Dahmer's pals said something about contacting Lucifer. When the lights dimmed and the candle sputtered, Geiger left and never saw Dahmer again. She can't recall if the party was before or after the date Dahmer gave for his first murder.

Martha Schmidt, who went to the senior prom with Mike Kukral, is now a sociology professor at Capital University in Columbus, Ohio. "He was tortured and lost at a very early age," she told reporters. "His behavior was always on the edge. He seemed to cry out for help, but nobody paid any attention to him at all."

On June 4, 1978, Jeffrey Dahmer graduated from Revere High School. Exactly two weeks later, he graduated into the sinister world of serial killers.

At the ten-year reunion of the class of 1978, classmates gathered to recall old times. Dahmer was a no-show, but someone mentioned his name.

"Hey, whatever happened to Jeff Dahmer?" someone asked.

"Oh, he's probably a mass murderer somewhere," somebody answered. They all laughed. But from what Dahmer told police, he had already killed four people by the time his classmates shared their joke back in Ohio.

4

First Blood

On June 18, 1978, Stephen Mark Hicks hitchhiked from his home in Coventry, Ohio, to a rock music concert thirty miles away at Chippewa Lake Park. That was the last his family saw of him.

He was looking forward to some summer vacation, kicking back a little before he decided what to do with the rest of his life. Four days shy of his nineteenth birthday, he had recently received his diploma from Coventry High School. Life was just beginning.

He was 5-foot-11, 160 pounds, with longish brown hair and a ready smile. He had on the uniform of the free spirit: blue jeans, blue sneakers, a neck chain with a red cross dangling from it.

Seeing Hicks hitchhiking, some high school buddies picked him up at 11 A.M. and drove him to the rock concert. There were tentative plans made to meet again that night for a party, but Hicks never showed.

He also failed to return home, but his family had grown accustomed to his staying out and didn't think much of it. As the days passed, however, his worried parents started calling friends to see if they had seen Stephen. They even called some hospitals. Maybe he had gotten hurt in an accident.

Six days later, his mother called the police, and the Summit County Sheriff's Department began compiling what would become an inch-thick missing-persons folder on Hicks.

Police retraced the hitchhiker's route, interviewed friends and acquaintances, and notified authorities in surrounding communities to see if he had turned up someplace else. Hicks's name, date of birth, and description were entered in a nationwide computer network designed to help find the missing.

It was as if he had vanished. Occasionally there were reports that someone had seen a man who looked like Hicks bagging groceries in a food store. Just another dead end.

If there were reports of unidentified bodies in

other parts of the country, the Hicks family sent dental records and other information. Still no luck.

The family offered a $2,500 reward. They hired a private investigator. In desperation they consulted a psychic, who tried but failed to contact Stephen spiritually.

As the years passed, the family's fears and worries turned into resignation. They had their son declared legally dead, but the sting of not knowing for sure kept the pain alive in their hearts.

They got the answer, which brought them more anguish than relief, from a hollow-eyed man in Milwaukee, who told police that the first of seventeen males he killed was an Ohio hitchhiker in 1978.

Summit County Detective John Karabatsos had worked on the Stephen Hicks case. When the information came from Milwaukee, he headed west with Bath Township Police Lieutenant Richard Munsey.

They talked with Jeffrey Dahmer for two and a half hours on July 27, and they never would have cracked the case if Dahmer hadn't cooperated. But that isn't to say Dahmer showed any guilt about his first blood.

When the Ohio officers showed him a picture of Stephen Hicks, Dahmer blankly said, "Yeah, that's him."

Hicks and Dahmer grew up fifteen miles apart, but had never met until Dahmer saw him thumbing along the Cleveland-Massillon Road in Bath Township after the concert. He picked him up near the Bath Township Police Department, of all places, which was about a mile from the Dahmer family's contemporary ranch-style home.

Dahmer was feeling deserted. His father had moved out during the bitter divorce proceeding, and his mother had taken his twelve-year-old brother away, leaving Jeffrey alone in a three-bedroom house.

Hicks accepted an offer to come over for a few beers, and they passed some time before Hicks got restless and decided to leave. Losing a companion, even one he had just met, was too much for Dahmer to bear. He felt abandoned by his parents, and he wasn't about to let anyone else walk out on him.

In a fit of murderous rage, Dahmer said, he picked up a barbell and smashed Hicks in the head, then used the bar to strangle him. The dying gasps and a racing pulse that stopped with death made a lasting impression; Dahmer had discovered a method of killing that he would repeat at least 16 more times.

In the statement the cops wrote down in his jail cell, Dahmer said, "The guy wanted to leave, and I didn't want him to leave." For having the simple desire to make his way home, Stephen Hicks was dead.

Now, what to do with a 160-pound body? Dahmer's mind was racing. He dragged the body outside to the entrance of a crawl space, an enclosed cavity between the cement-block foundation and the bedrock on which the Dahmer house was built. Dahmer and his childhood chums played in there, and it was sometimes used for storage.

According to statements he gave police, Dahmer used a kitchen knife to cut Hicks apart inside the crawl space, stuffing the pieces into large plastic bags. He put the bags in the car, figuring he'd toss them away somewhere, then changed his mind and decided to bury them in the backyard near a drainpipe. It was tough digging in the rocky, craggy soil; and all he managed to gouge out was a shallow grave.

Something gnawed at him. What if the grave was discovered? Then he had a better idea. He looked to his clubhouse, where he learned how acid melts flesh from animal bones. The same stuff would consume human remains. Over the next two weeks, Dahmer went to work, stripping away the skin, muscle, and tissue.

Next he took a sledgehammer and pounded away at the skull, backbone, ribs, arms, and legs. He smashed the body into hundreds of pieces, none bigger than the size of a hand. It was as if all the pent-up emotion inside was released with those blows.

When the hammering stopped, Dahmer gathered

the fragments and took them out back. Turning in a circle, he scattered them to be absorbed by the soil.

To get rid of the knife he used to hack apart the body, Dahmer pitched it from a bridge on Bath Road into the Cuyahoga River. He also discarded Hicks's necklace and burned his wallet.

Thirteen years later, long after the Dahmer estate had been settled and sold, the new owner would see the property take on the look of an archeological dig. Indeed, one of those helping the authorities was a Kent State University anthropologist, C. Owen Lovejoy. He is best known for his studies of a four-million-year-old fossil named Lucy, a bit of bone that might shed some light on the origins of the human race.

Also serving as a consultant was Robert Mann, a physical anthropologist from the Smithsonian Institution—among other things, a repository for the origins of humans, animals, and insects. The idea was to piece together the bones, like pieces of a puzzle, and reconstruct the body. The painstaking work would confirm Hicks's identity and make sure no one else was scattered out there.

Police sealed off the area with yellow tape, then divided the yard into grids marked with red ribbons and wooden stakes before going to work. Dahmer had drawn them a map of where he had scattered the bones.

In the crawl space, technicians wearing masks

over their mouths and noses sprayed a chemical called Luminol, a staple of crime investigators. When Luminol comes in contact with blood, it glows in a greenish hue, something like the tail of a lightning bug. Even thirteen-year-old blood will react.

To the naked eye, the cinder blocks were bare. But with the Luminol mist applied from plastic squirt bottles, a bloody handprint emerged. On the bedrock floor, large pools of dried blood glowed. More evidence of Dahmer's deeds.

In the yard, a twenty-five-man search team raked the soil, inch by inch, for bone fragments. The more they worked, the more they learned. Police started digging two to six inches deep into the rocky soil, sifting the scoops with screens to yield more pieces.

In a week's worth of labors, authorities had inventoried 593 items—hundreds of bone fragments, pieces of two incisors, a fragment of a molar, finger bones, and other things, each placed in a clear plastic bag. One find spoke of Dahmer's early hobbies: it was a glass jar containing rodent bones.

"He was very thorough with that sledgehammer," noted William A. Cox, the Summit County coroner.

Cox is a forensic pathologist who was the chief of pathology at the Westover Air Force Base hospital in Massachusetts during the Vietnam War. He

later received more training at the Armed Forces
Institute of Pathology, where military specialists are
trained to identify battlefield dead from the smallest
traces of fragments. He also studied at the Smithsonian.

His work is dispassionately clinical, taking
pieces and rebuilding them into a picture that tells a
story. But Cox was not one to lose sight that this
was a human story too.

"Everything we do is to make a scientific deter-
mination," Cox said. "But at the same time, you
keep in the back of your mind that this was once a
living, breathing human being. There are people out
there who loved him. The family has asked for the
remains to be returned back to them. And we're
going to do that. So they can pay their last respects."

The Hicks family had saved a lock of their son's
hair, hoping that someday they could use it to
genetically match any of his remains if they were
found. Now they had their answer, after thirteen
long, painful years. There were no more straws of
hope to grasp.

In a statement issued after the discovery, the
family said, "He had qualities that would make any
parent proud. He also had problems not uncommon
to youth of that time: drinking, smoking, traffic
tickets, and the occasional rowdiness of youth.

"Dahmer's actions have altered our lives forever," the family said.

"As a family, we have spent a great deal of time trying to understand the motivation for such a heinous crime and concluded that some acts are so evil they simply cannot be explained."

In an interview with the *Akron Beacon Journal,* Richard Hicks said of Dahmer, "Is he insane? In my opinion, no. He is evil. If I thought killing would bring my son back, I would do it myself."

The family asked to be left alone so that they could grieve in private. Sixteen other families would later sense the depth of the Hickses' misery.

Meanwhile, Ohio authorities made it clear they would leave no stone unturned in gathering evidence and verifying statements made by Dahmer, no matter what he had confessed to and how much he had cooperated. "This is the type of person you want to see prosecuted for every offense," said Lynn Slaby, the district attorney in Summit County.

Slaby noted the cold, calculating precision of Dahmer's work, the thought processes that went into his chores. "I feel strongly he was not acting as a criminally insane person. His acts were deliberate. He hid the body. That clearly indicates that he knew that what he did was wrong," Slaby said.

Bath Township Police Captain John Gardner, the shepherd of 9,015 residents in his jurisdiction, had a full-scale media invasion on his hands. In his twenty-one years on the force, he had investigated only five murders. His normal caseload is ten drunk driving arrests a month, maybe five burglaries a month, and a robbery every six months.

A roadside tomato stand reveals much about Bath Township. An enterprising gardener places baskets of the ripe red delicacies out on a bench. The price for a basket is noted at $2.50, and a sign tells customers to make their own change from a jar of cash. Customers pull up, buy tomatoes, and drive off. But it's all done on the honor system. The seller stays in the house, not worried that anyone is cheating or stealing tomatoes.

But just down the road, there were two hundred reporters from around the country clamoring for news about a thirteen-year-old murder. Eight satellite trucks lined the street. Two news helicopters hovered overhead.

The police set up a portable toilet for the media horde.

From a driveway, Leena Tripp, thirteen, and Stacy Staats, twelve, sold coffee, cookies, and lemonade from their stand.

"It's horrible that somebody would do something like that. It gives the town a real bad reputation," Stacy Staats said.

Ohio authorities planned to convene a grand jury to press ahead with the criminal investigation. But any prosecution of Dahmer would wait until the cases in Wisconsin were resolved.

5

Restlessness—
And Death

The summer of 1978 had been a tragically eventful one for Jeffrey Dahmer: the Stephen Hicks episode; his mother moving away with his twelve-year-old brother; his father having long since moved out; the divorce becoming final. Now it was on to college.

Dahmer's one semester at Ohio State University, where he hoped to major in business, ended with his quitting.

His father recalled Dahmer's Morrill Tower dormitory room lined with empty bottles. Dahmer peddled his plasma at a Columbus blood bank, using the money to feed his alcohol habit.

His roommate, Michael Prochaska, of Cleveland, told the *Ohio State Lantern* that Dahmer "used to take bottles to class with him and came back drunk." He was a loner and got no mail from home.

There was a theft of a watch, a radio, and $120 from another resident in his dorm. Campus police questioned Dahmer as a suspect. No charges were filed.

Martha Schmidt figured he was beyond help when she saw him passed out on a Columbus street.

Such credentials offer few career opportunities, so Dahmer enlisted in the U.S. Army. On December 29, 1978, five days after his father married Shari Jordan, Dahmer raised his right hand and began a three-year commitment. His father went with him to the induction, hoping some drill sergeant or army discipline could straighten out a son that he had failed to straighten out. To a neighbor, Lionel Dahmer described the army as "that government babysitter."

Dahmer's school chums were bemused by it all.

"We'd heard he joined the army. We joked that he was America's secret weapon. We could all feel safe now because Dahmer was in the army," said Mike Kukral.

He took basic training at Fort McClellan in Anniston, Alabama, and hoped to become a military policeman. But he didn't last with the MPs, and he was reassigned as a medical specialist. He got his training at Fort Sam Houston in San Antonio, Texas.

On July 13, 1979, he received orders to report to Baumholder, West Germany, to serve as a combat medic at a medical aid station with the 2nd Battalion. He was the military's version of a nurse's aide.

But it wasn't long before the alcohol pattern resurfaced.

The enlisted men in Dahmer's unit bunked in two rooms, each one sleeping eight soldiers. Dennis Rodriguez and Michael Masters roomed with him for his final year in the service.

What they remember in connection with Dahmer was a briefcase set up as a portable bar—something that he could keep his liquor in and not be caught by his superiors. It was an elaborate case—martini mixers, shakers, stirrers, glasses, and flasks. He made dry martinis from Beefeater gin, put on his Black Sabbath tapes, and closed himself off during his weekend binges.

"He would drink and have his headphones on, kind of be shut out from the rest of the world," Rodriguez said. "He wouldn't move. He wouldn't even go out for chow. He wouldn't get takeout food. He'd drink until he passed out and then wake up and drink some more. There were a lot of people who used to drink, but not like him.''

Once, when Dahmer passed out from the alcohol, his roommates put an empty bottle of Thunderbird next to him and snapped a picture. But Dahmer never drank wine, just the hard stuff.

On weekdays, Rodriguez remembered Dahmer taking his "briefcase" to the library and coming back late at night. Sometimes he'd be gone for an entire weekend—from the time he got off duty on Friday to when he reported to the aid station on Monday.

The army was in a transition phase at the time, just beginning a rebuilding effort. Eventually, the professional soldiers who cared enough to shape up demoralized ranks produced the fighting force that humiliated Saddam Hussein's troops in the Persian Gulf. But back then the stain of Vietnam was fresher, and wearing a uniform wasn't the most popular thing to do in the late 1970s. The draft was long gone, but among the volunteers who entered the military were a goodly number of misfits, losers, and loners who had no place else to go in life. They were people looking for an extended family.

This is where Dahmer, a private first class, sought to find a niche for himself. A quiet loner who sometimes played chess, he didn't cause problems for anybody else, except for his belligerence when drinking. He never mentioned his family. Never got any mail. Never distinguished himself. Never took the initiative. Just slid by with his army work.

"He always had that look about him, something sinister," said Michael Masters. "He would never explode. He never showed anger. He would never act it out. He was very calculating. I don't know, he was on a steady decline in life. He was on a losing skid and didn't know how to pick himself up."

One more thing. When Dahmer was drinking, he'd make racist remarks to black soldiers. One of them, Billy Capshaw, of Hot Springs, Arkansas, said Dahmer once gave him a birthday card, but on other occasions gave him nothing but hard times.

"I knew for a fact he was gonna hurt me if he ever got hold of me," said Capshaw, now serving a one-year sentence in the Garland County Jail in Hot Springs, Arkansas, for a misdemeanor of negligent homicide (a fourteen-year-old borrowed his car and hit and killed someone). "He'd run after you like a crazy man, like a wild nut."

When the news from Milwaukee flashed around the world, authorities in Germany took another look at nine unsolved murder cases that occurred when Dahmer was at Baumholder.

There were no immediate links, said Helmut Bleh, a state prosecutor in Bad Kreuznach who had hoped to clear up the death of a twenty-two-year-old female hitchhiker who was stabbed and strangled in November of 1980. She was found frozen in the early snows about thirty miles from Baumholder, her hands bound with cord.

In Dahmer's final months in the army, his fellow soldiers said his drinking got worse and his work, always considered marginal, suffered. Colleagues said he had liquor on his breath when he reported in the morning. He showed up late, then stopped showing up at all. Nine months short of fulfilling his contract, Dahmer was discharged under Chapter 9 of the Uniform Code of Military Justice—the section that deals with alcohol and drug abuse. Still a private first class after more than two years in the army, he was let go on March 26, 1981.

Dahmer's squad leader, David D. Goss, drove him to the airport for the trip back to the United States. "There was something that was bugging him in Germany," Goss later told reporters. "I knew he had a troubled past and I knew he had something that was gnawing at him. . . . He'd say there was something he could not talk about."

But Dahmer did blurt something out as he prepared to exit the army and end another failed chapter in his life: "Some day," he told colleagues, "you'll hear about me again."

Back in the States, Dahmer headed for the sunny climes of Miami, Florida. He worked in a sandwich shop and slept on Miami Beach. He lasted about six months before he headed back to Ohio.

Later, authorities in Hollywood, Florida, wanted to know if Dahmer had any connection to the murder of Adam Walsh. The six-year-old was abducted from a shopping mall on July 27, 1981; two weeks later the boy's head was found in a Vero Beach canal, 120 miles away. The case remains unsolved.

Authorities in California, Kansas, Missouri, Michigan, and just about every other place where police had found dismembered victims wanted to talk to him. At one point, the Milwaukee police were receiving a call every thirty seconds from someone wanting to know if Dahmer could have been connected to a particular crime.

From his jail cell, Dahmer denied killing anyone outside Ohio or Wisconsin. In a statement issued through his attorney, he said, "I have told the police everything I have done relative to these homicides. I have not committed any such crimes anywhere in the world other than this state, except I have admitted an incident in Ohio. I have been totally cooperative and I would have admitted other crimes if I did them. I did not. Hopefully this will put rumors to rest."

From Florida, Dahmer moved back to Ohio. Neighbors said he spoke of joining the FBI, but troubles percolated to the surface once again.

On October 7, he was arrested by Bath Township police and charged with disorderly conduct and resisting arrest. He was fined sixty dollars, but his ten-day jail term was suspended. According to police, Dahmer had gone to Maxwell's Lounge at the Ramada Inn with an open bottle of vodka. Police were called, and they said Dahmer refused to get in the squad car when they came to take him away.

His father noticed an emerging pattern linked to drinking. Dahmer would borrow the family car, then get drunk and forget where he left it. He became a fixture at bars, staying till closing time and then getting nasty when he was told to leave.

It was time for a change.

In early 1982, Dahmer went to live with his grandmother, Catherine, in the well-kept Milwaukee suburb of West Allis. Yet the pattern continued.

"He roamed around the bars and repeatedly stayed until time, then he'd demand more drinks," Lionel Dahmer told reporters. "They'd usher him out. Sometimes there'd be fights. He'd get hurt badly. He was attacked several times and had stitches over his eye and broken ribs.

"This was probably very wrong to do, but I didn't have the wisdom to do anything differently, and we sent him to his grandmother's to live. A new scene. They loved each other, and he'd help her with the chores."

Catherine Dahmer seemed to be the one person

who had some kind of emotional connection to her
troubled grandson. Maybe it was because she paid
attention when he felt neglected, or she soothed him
when he needed a pat on the head. She sent him
greeting cards on his birthday and other holidays.
Like good grandmas do, she sent money too. Even
long after he had moved out and got in big trouble
with the law, Catherine Dahmer would drive to a
tough Milwaukee neighborhood to take her grandson to places that repaired his fish tank.

"He had an awful lot of love for me. He never
left without giving me a big hug," his grandmother
told reporters the day after his arrest. "He always
wanted to do things for me."

Dahmer found some solace in West Allis. He
mowed his grandmother's grass, helped her plant
roses, trimmed the shrubs, raked the leaves that fell
on a patch of lawn surrounding a neat, two-story
frame house.

He left behind the bickering parents, the past
failures, the proximity of the Stephen Mark Hicks
episode. And he enjoyed freedom. His grandmother's house had a side entrance that led down to the
basement or up to the kitchen. He could come and
go as he pleased, and he could bring home guests
for intimate encounters.

Dahmer had always had trouble getting close to
people. Now he was in a new town, a cold town
where he didn't know anyone. He was also troubled

by his sexuality. He was never comfortable with girls, but he stayed deep in the closet with his homosexuality.

Eventually, he discovered the gay bars on Milwaukee's south side. The area is an industrial one in transition to gentrification, dotted with watering holes and social hangouts. But not long ago it was called the "gay ghetto."

Regulars in the bars said Dahmer was not a great socializer. He sat and drank alone, and nobody hassled him.

Gay clubs are like social centers. Their patrons feel spurned or even persecuted for their sexual orientation by most of society, sometimes by their own families. If they feel out of place, if nobody else wants them around, or if they feel uncomfortable with their sexual feelings, they can feel at home among others like them. A gay club is a chance to meet friends, dance, laugh, exchange views, pick up lovers. It is a separate little world, one that insulates patrons from the gay-bashers. The regulars share a common bond of sexuality; and a feeling of trust emerged among the people who frequented Club 219, the Phoenix, C'est La Vie, and the other bars. That trust eventually led some of them to be betrayed, however. They were too eager to embrace the quiet loner with the sandy hair who asked them if they wanted to come back to his grandmother's house for a drink.

Dahmer didn't stay trouble-free for long.

On August 8, 1982, Dahmer was arrested by police at the Wisconsin State Fair Park, a festive place where midwestern families come for weekend flea markets, arts and crafts shows, and ethnic music festivals where they can tap their toes to the oom-pah-pah of polkas and happily consume their bratwurst and beer. He was charged with disorderly conduct and paid a fifty-dollar fine. According to the police report, "Dahmer did lower his pants in the presence of approximately twenty-five people, including women and children."

At the time, he was working at the Wisconsin Blood Plasma Center, drawing blood from donors.

Lowering his pants appeared to be becoming another of his traits, just as "doing a Dahmer" was a high-school hallmark.

On August 8, 1986, Milwaukee police charged Dahmer with lewd and lascivious behavior. Two twelve-year-old boys said they saw Dahmer, with his pants pulled down around his thighs, masturbating on the banks of the Kinnickinnic River, which winds its way to Lake Michigan and is a popular frolicking ground for kids.

According to news accounts, when one of the boys asked him if he was having a good time, Dahmer replied, "Yeah, I'm having a great time."

In the police report, the arresting officer said

Dahmer admitted masturbating in public about five times in the preceding months. "He doesn't know what changed him to make him suddenly start doing this, and that he knows he has a problem and he wants to get help," the officer said in his report.

Six months later, the charge was reduced to disorderly conduct and Dahmer was placed on a year's probation.

He gave a far different account to his probation officer, saying he was drinking alone in a wooded area along the riverbank. "After a few cans of beer, I needed to go, so I did, behind some trees. I was sure there was no one else around, but I was wrong. Two boys saw me and called the police," Dahmer stated.

The agent from the state division of probation and parole noted that Dahmer was dissatisfied with his family, with himself, and with the turbulence of his childhood. Dahmer had no close friends and didn't trust people. The agent figured family problems and childhood emotional factors contributed to Dahmer's inability to have a normal social life.

Dahmer said he had thought about killing himself. The agent's notes read, "Carbon dioxide. Always an alternative."

And when asked about his job skills, Dahmer, who began working two years earlier for the Ambrosia Chocolate Company, wrote: "I know how to

mix chocolate—that's about it. Some medical training in the army.''

There were two more minor run-ins with the
cops. Both involved allegations that Dahmer had
drugged companions, but criminal charges weren't
filed in either case.

In the summer of 1986, Dahmer was barred from
Club Baths, a gay bathhouse and pickup joint in
Milwaukee. Owners said he slipped drugged drinks
to at least four patrons there. He'd bring them into
a private stall, then offer an alcoholic beverage.

"We had to kick Dahmer out because he was
drugging people in his private room. I didn't want
to deal with that," Bradley Babush, a former manager of Club Baths, told the press. "One person
from Madison was unconscious and we couldn't
revive him. We called the paramedics and they took
him to the hospital. He was in the hospital for a
week to ten days."

The police questioned the staff and Dahmer
about the incident. No one wanted to press charges.

At Club Baths, it was common practice for men
to walk around in their towels, pair up with willing
partners and head to a stall. In 1988, city health
authorities closed Club Baths, which was similar to
the gay bathhouses popular in San Francisco and
New York. They cited concerns over a possible
tuberculosis outbreak there. Other cities have

closed bathhouses because unsafe sexual practices were contributing to the spread of AIDS.

Apparently, Dahmer was not deterred. In April of 1988, Ronald D. Flowers of Zion, Illinois, said he met Dahmer at a gay bar on Milwaukee's south side. They went back to Dahmer's grandmother's house in West Allis, where Flowers claimed Dahmer gave him a spiked drink. He told police he woke up the next day at the Milwaukee County Medical Complex in Wauwatosa, minus the cash from his wallet and a gold bracelet from his wrist.

When West Allis police came to question him, Dahmer said he and his male companion merely drank until they passed out. Then in the morning, with Flowers still intoxicated, Dahmer escorted the man to a bus stop and gave him a dollar for a fare.

Police didn't have enough to go on to press any charges. No traces of knockout drugs were found in Flowers's system, and Dahmer's grandmother said she saw her grandson walking a man to the bus stop.

It was dropped.

In retrospect, Flowers was as lucky as Tracy Edwards, although he never got slapped with handcuffs. By the time of his encounter with Flowers, Dahmer had already murdered four times. The next time West Allis police had contact with Dahmer, he admitted that he picked up men in gay bars, brought them back to his grandmother's house, drugged them, killed them, and then disposed of their bodies.

Catherine Dahmer noticed some awful smells coming from her garage.

At Catherine's request, Lionel Dahmer came out to investigate, although a lot of what had been in the garage had been set out with the garbage. Inside, he told reporters, he found "a little slimy black viscous residue."

He recounted for reporters a confrontation he had had with his son. "He said, 'I just had too much time on my hands and I just wanted to see what chemicals would decompose the chicken I bought.' "

Dahmer also confessed to his father that while riding the bus home one day he spied a dead raccoon. It was just like the road kills he used to pick up from the country lanes of northwestern Ohio. So he got off the bus and brought it home to experiment with.

"I said, 'God, Jeff. This is strange. This is weird,' " Lionel Dahmer said.

Later it was learned that the odors had another probable source. Dahmer told police he killed three men inside his grandmother's home, then melted down the bodies in acid.

But to his father he explained away the smells as

convincingly as he told later neighbors his groceries were spoiled or his fish tank was acting up.

He had developed a convincing way of talking his way out of trouble, and Lionel Dahmer was aware of it. "Jeff would lie, and we'd catch him in lies. At other times he would be absolutely frank, and I'd check up and find him to be frank. You can't tell with a person like that whether you're getting the truth or not," his father told reporters.

"I've always felt he was somewhat of a social misfit," he said. "I tried my damnedest to instill interests, in trying to become interested in something in life, education, trying to get him to accept Christ."

Dahmer already had interests, however. And things were getting out of hand at Grandma's house. According to Shari Dahmer, his stepmother, one time his grandmother started to come down to the basement, but her grandson was engaged in some kind of activity with a male companion. She thought they were undressed.

In an interview with *The Plain Dealer* of Cleveland, Shari Dahmer said he told the woman, "Don't come down here. You don't want to come down here."

6

Victims

The accounts of Jeffrey Dahmer's deeds come from his own mouth. There are no known witnesses, and in some cases there is no physical evidence to verify the statements written down by police. The district attorney has charged him with fifteen counts of first-degree intentional homocide.

Jeffrey Dahmer told police he killed his first Wisconsin victim in November of 1987, nine years and five months after his encounter with Stephen Hicks in Ohio. He was living with his grandmother in West Allis at the time.

Details are sketchiest in this case. It involves twenty-four-year-old Steven W. Tuomi, whose parents in Ontonagon, Michigan, reported he disappeared on September 15.

Tuomi's case is the only one in Wisconsin in which murder charges will not be filed. Milwaukee County District Attorney E. Michael McCann said he brought charges only in cases he felt could be proven beyond a reasonable doubt.

"All we have to go on is what Dahmer told us. There is no physical evidence," said Robert Due, deputy chief of the West Allis Police Department. "Dahmer doesn't know how he died. He woke up in a hotel room and this guy was dead."

The *New York Times* quoted police reports as saying Dahmer met his first Wisconsin victim at Club 219 and they went to the Ambassador Hotel, where a room for two costs $43.88. There was a separate charge of $10 for the room key, refundable at checkout time.

Dahmer said they drank until they passed out. "When he woke up, the guy was dead and had blood coming from his mouth." the police report said.

Leaving the body in the room, Dahmer went to a nearby mall and bought a large suitcase, to stuff the body inside. He called a taxi and took it to his grandmother's house, with the cabbie lending a hand with the heavy bag. Once there, he cut up the body and disposed of it. Tuomi was gone without a trace, and no remains were ever found. There is only Dahmer's word that the episode happened at all.

The regulars in the gay bars had noticed that a light-haired patron named Steve had stopped coming around and wondered if something had happened to him.

"Yeah, there was a kid missing named Steve. I don't know his last name," said John Taylor, owner of C'est La Vie. "All of a sudden, friends that have been missing are dead, it's quite a shock."

The *Times* account, based on the police report, surprised authorities because none of that information had been made public.

Subsequently, authorities said that an $8.30-an-hour janitor who cleans the district attorney's office photocopied some documents and delivered them to the newspaper. The *Times* denied doing anything underhanded and said it did not pay for the documents and that the reporter believed he was getting information obtained from legitimate sources.

Supervisors suspended Stephen Dean Sessions, twenty-nine, who has done janitorial work for Milwaukee County since 1988, and asked for his firing. He was charged with violating a civil service rule banning employees from obtaining or disclosing confidential or privileged information.

"Shame on the *New York Times*," said prosecutor McCann. "While the extensive media attention given this case is understandable, every professional ought to act responsibly. The public has a right to know, but it also has a right to believe that fair trials will not be thwarted and criminal investigations will not be compromised by overzealous media.''

The report copied by the janitor said Dahmer fried the biceps of a victim in vegetable shortening and ate them.

It also said Dahmer once consulted with a hardware store about what chemical would best preserve a rabbit pelt. The store recommended acetone, which Dahmer said he then used to save a victim's scalp and ponytail.

Also according to the report: ''Subject states that the body parts gave off an awful smell in the trash, but no one ever did anything, so he just kept following his usual procedure.''

James Doxtator was fourteen years old. He was a regular at the bus stop outside Club 219. Teens who stood out there sold themselves for sexual favors to the men who cruised by. They allowed the exploitation of the one thing of value they had, the one thing other men wanted: their bodies. One night in January of 1988. Dahmer approached Doxtator and said hello. Dahmer asked the boy if he'd like to come over for a drink. They could watch some videos, and Dahmer said he'd pay cash if the boy posed nude for some pictures. Dahmer thought the boy was Hispanic, but he was a Native American.

The two rode the bus to West Allis, and Dahmer said they had sex in the basement. Dahmer told police he then drugged the boy, strangled him, and dismembered him. Echoes must have sounded in his mind from the encounter with Ohio hitchhiker Stephen Hicks ten years earlier. Dahmer cleaned the flesh from Doxtator's bones with acid, then smashed the bones with a sledgehammer. He pounded and pounded, crushing up legs and arms and ribs and spine and skull, until they were small enough to discard. He didn't save anything, and the whereabouts of the bone fragments are unknown. Another stranger's life was obliterated without a trace.

There was one remarkable feature about Doxtator that Dahmer remembered. It helped police identify the victim. The boy had two scars near his nipples that looked like cigarette burns.

Doxtator's mother, Debra Vega, told police her son had scars like that on his chest. She said she last saw her son on January 16, 1988, and thought he had run away.

She moved from Milwaukee to Florida last year to start life anew. "He needs to suffer and suffer and suffer, just like the families and the victims he has hurt," Vega said of Dahmer.

Vega said West Allis police had asked her to

send them a picture of her son. When shown the picture of Doxtator, Dahmer told police he was 75 percent certain it was the boy he killed.

Two months later, Dahmer said, he met a Hispanic man in the Phoenix Bar, located on the same street as Club 219. The family of Richard Guerrero said he disappeared on March 24, 1988, with three dollars in his pocket and no wallet.

Dahmer made a proposition: come back to the house in West Allis, watch some videos, take some pictures in the nude, and have sex. Back at his grandmother's house, Dahmer told police, the two of them had oral sex. He then drugged Guerrero, killed him, cut up the body, and got rid of all of it.

He remembered the man because he later saw a missing person report in the local paper. The notices were placed there by the victim's worried family.

The family did all they could to find their son. Four months after Richard disappeared, the Guerreros hired a private investigator. He found nothing but dead ends. They printed flyers with Richard's picture and description, a 5-foot-6, 130-pound male with thick, dark hair. The combed the banks of the Milwaukee River, thinking they might find a body that washed ashore. They wrote to the TV show *Unsolved Mysteries*. They hired a psychic, someone who claimed he might learn of Richard's where-

abouts by touching his clothing and belongings.
Every few months, for the past three years, someone called the police to see if there had been any
progress. Once, they said, they were told by police,
"He's not the only missing person out there."

"We tried everything we could," Richard's father, Pablo, said.

Their desperate search was remindful of the
futile efforts made by the family of Stephen Hicks
in Coventry, Ohio. The family posted a reward,
hired a private eye, and consulted a psychic.

"Understand that in thirteen years we've
grabbed at some straws," Richard Hicks told Cleveland television station WKYC. "We're not ignorant
people. We're well-read people. But driven to frus-
tration by not knowing—and the desperation . . ."

When Richard's family heard through the media
how Dahmer lured victims with promises of money,
their fears escalated.

"When you're young and at a bar and you run
out of money, you run into a guy who has beer at
home, so you go," figured Pablo. Soon their fears
would be confirmed.

Sounthome Sinthasomphone came to America
with his wife and eight children to escape death.

He was a rice farmer in Laos, one of the poorest
countries on earth, where yearly per capita income
is $170 and the life expectancy is forty-five years.

Laos had fallen to the communist Pathet Lao guerrillas in 1975. It was part of the debacle in Indochina where, despite a decade of American intervention, despite American blood and dollars and military might, Saigon fell to North Vietnam, also in 1975.

In Laos, the communists sent U.S. sympathizers to resettlement camps and reeducation centers. Most never returned. They were victims of bloody crackdowns and purges. Whole families disappeared because they were suspected of having the wrong political ideology.

From 1975 to 1980, more than 300,000 refugees—10 percent of the country's population—fled the bloodshed. Among them was Sinthasomphone, who feared the government was about to seize his rice farm in a village near the capital of Vientiane on the Mekong River. Laos runs on a rice economy, and the government was collectivizing the paddies, to be run by the central government.

Sinthasomphone faced an uncertain future in a strange country where he knew neither the customs nor the language. But he figured it was worth the risk if he could find freedom, justice, and safety for his wife, Somdy, and their eight children.

He built a boat and packed his family into it for a nighttime trip across the Mekong River into Thailand. He said he gave the children sedatives so that they wouldn't cry out and attract communist guards. Among those huddled in the boat was three-year-old Konerak, the baby of the family.

The ragtag group first came to the Nonkai refugee resettlement camp, where a human torrent from Laos and Cambodia pooled into Thailand. The family stayed for a year, eventually hooking up with representatives of American-based refugee relocation programs. One of the groups offering help was the Catholic Archdiocese in a strange-sounding place called Milwaukee, a word in the Algonquin Indian language that means good place. In 1980, they arrived in the heartland of America. It was a sharp contrast to Southeast Asia, what with the bitter winter winds off Lake Michigan, the ethnic groups who drank their beer and ate bratwurst with gusto, and the cream-colored concrete-and-glass buildings that replaced the farm fields of Laos. But it was a workingman's town, with blue-collar ethnic neighborhoods. About seven thousand Laotians had resettled here. It offered the promise of a second chance. Better yet, it had no communist thugs butchering the population.

Barely ten years later, Sinthasomphone would know all he'd ever care to about crime in America.

Dahmer had outgrown his grandmother's house. His carousing with men, his drinking, and his strange hours were too much for an aging woman. So he scouted around for his own place, settling on an apartment at 808 N. 24th St. on Milwaukee's west side. His family believes the day he moved in was the day he first devastated the Sinthasomphone family.

A thirteen-year-old boy was walking home from school on September 25, 1988, when Dahmer approached him. The sandy-haired man who worked at a chocolate factory told the boy he had just purchased a new camera, and he was willing to pay fifty dollars if the boy would come over to his place and pose for pictures.

Fifty bucks to an immigrant Asian kid without much money sounded pretty good. In the apartment, Dahmer offered a cup of coffee. The criminal complaint filed against Dahmer said he spiked the brown liquid with the sleeping pill Halcion, a prescription drug that comes from the class of tranquilizers known as benzodiazepine. A similar substance was found in Oliver Lacy, whose head was later found in Dahmer's refrigerator.

Dahmer posed the boy for pictures, reached down with his hand to fondle the boy's genitals, and asked him to "look sexier for the pose." With other men, the drug would knock them out and render them helpless, allowing Dahmer to do as he pleased.

The full scene wasn't played out this time. Somehow, the staggering boy escaped and ended up in a hospital. On January 30, 1989. Dahmer was convicted in circuit court of the felony charges of second-degree sexual assault and enticing a child for immoral purposes. It was a conviction for which he would serve less than a year behind bars.

The conviction wasn't about to stop Dahmer. Just two months after his conviction and two months before he was sentenced, he was at it again back at his grandmother's house.

Anthony Sears, twenty-six, told his mother he'd be over for dinner on March 26, 1989—Easter Sunday. He never made it.

"He'd often make plans with me, and then go off and do something with his friends. I didn't think much of it at first," said his mother, Marilyn.

She said he was an outgoing sort who talked of being a model. "He loved to have his picture taken," she said.

Sears encountered Dahmer the night before. Sears was celebrating his recent promotion as manager of Baker's Square restaurant with a friend, Jeffrey Connor, at a bar called La Cage in downtown Milwaukee.

During the evening, Sears met a white male named Jeff, who said he was from Chicago and visiting his grandparents in West Allis. Jeff invited him over for a nightcap.

Connor told Milwaukee police he dropped the two of them off at 56th Street and Lincoln, which is just a short distance from the home of Dahmer's grandmother at 2357 S. 57th St. They headed south, and that was the last Connor saw of Sears.

Dahmer told police he had sex with Sears, then gave him a drink with a sleeping potion in it. He strangled Sears and dismembered the body. This time, he decided to keep the skull as a memento. He boiled the head to remove the skin, then painted it to preserve it. It was the beginning of a macabre collection of human souvenirs.

He later took the skull when he moved into his second apartment, at the Oxford complex, where police found it July 22, 1991.

After Dahmer's admissions. West Allis police searched his grandmother's house and garage. They confiscated a sledgehammer, a hatchet, a sewer grate, and several bottles of prescription sleeping pills.

Meanwhile, Mrs. Sears had learned that her son was last seen with another man in West Allis. A mother's intuition confirmed her worst fears. "When I saw Dahmer's grandmother's house on TV, I knew he had been killed there," she said.

Mrs. Sears said her son's girlfriend left Milwaukee a year ago, unable to come to grips with his vanishing from sight.

At an August 8, 1991 memorial service, a picture of Anthony Sears stood under a wreath of flowers at the altar of Christ Memorial Church of God in Christ. Marilyn Sears, the mother of fifteen children, left the church with a sense of tranquility she had not known for two years.

"Now I can be at peace," she said.

Jeffrey Dahmer was back in court on May 23, 1989, before Circuit Judge William D. Gardner, to be sentenced on his conviction of second-degree sexual assault and enticing a child for immoral purposes. The prosecutor in the case, assistant district attorney Gale Shelton, urged the judge to send Dahmer to prison.

Shelton has worked in the district attorney's office for eleven years, the last six of them in the sensitive-crimes unit. She was especially disturbed by Dahmer's claim that the sedative was a residue inadvertently left in a coffee cup. She figured Dahmer's behavior would happen again and again if he went unpunished.

"The thing that stood out in my mind was that people who commit sexual assault against children almost never use drugs. Kids are trusting. They do what you say. That was a real red flag," Shelton said.

She also said Dahmer had "a disturbing profile" because he didn't try to atone for his mistake.

According to court transcripts, Shelton told the judge that Dahmer preyed on the thirteen-year-old boy "because he looked like a soft-spoken young man who could be easily victimized. Mr. Dahmer knew full well he was not dealing with a consenting adult. The boy indicated that within a short time of drinking the coffee that he immediately felt woozy."

She continued, "It's really a miracle he made it out of there." She could not have known how accurate she was.

In her arguments for a prison sentence, Gale Shelton noted that Dahmer merely "went through the motions" in therapy after getting probation for the disorderly conduct charge in 1986.

"In my judgment, it is absolutely crystal clear that the prognosis for treatment of Mr. Dahmer within the community is extremely bleak . . . and is just plain not going to work," she had said.

"That's absolutely clear from every single professional who's looked at Mr. Dahmer, and the reality is that his track record exhibits that he is very likely to reoffend."

Shelton spoke of Dahmer's "deep-seated anger and deep-seated psychological problems that . . . he's apparently completely unwilling or incapable of dealing with."

She called Dahmer evasive, uncooperative, manipulative, and unwilling to change. To help him and to protect society, it would be best to treat Dahmer in prison for his ills, Shelton said.

Dahmer's lawyer that day was Gerald Boyle, the attorney who the day after the discoveries in his client's apartment said Dahmer wanted to come clean.

Boyle argued for leniency.

"It happened on one occasion," Boyle said of the crime. "We know pretty well that since that time in September of last year, he has been functioning in this society without any intense kind of psychological or alcoholic help, and he hasn't done anything like it again."

Without Boyle's realizing it at the time, Anthony Sears's skull was back at Catherine Dahmer's house in West Allis.

Boyle argued that Dahmer's best chance of rehabilitating himself was to get treatment in the private community instead of a prison sentence.

"He's very alone in the world, your Honor. He really is monastic and Spartan, the way he conducts the affairs of his life, which is probably nobody's fault but his own," Boyle said.

"We don't have a multiple offender here. I believe he was caught before it got to the point where it would have gotten worse."

What Boyle and the court didn't know was that Dahmer would later admit to having killed five times before the hearing.

Lionel Dahmer, in a letter that became part of the court record, also asked that his son get treatment instead of a prison uniform.

Then it was Jeffrey Dahmer's turn to speak for

himself. Judge Gardner wanted to know more about him, and Dahmer gave a convincing performance. He began by saying he had a drinking problem and was a homosexual with sexual problems. He begged for another chance, promising never to stray again.

"I am an alcoholic. Not the sort that has to have a drink every single day, but when I do drink, I go overboard," Dahmer said.

"The prosecution has raised very serious charges against me, and I can understand why. What I've done is very serious. I never meant to give anyone the impression that I thought otherwise. I've never been in this position before. Nothing this awful. This is a nightmare come true for me. If anything would shock me out of my past behavior patterns, it's this," he continued.

Dahmer also said the best thing he had going for him was his $8.25-an-hour job at the Ambrosia Chocolate Co., where he was hired on January 14, 1985. A work-release sentence would allow him to keep it.

"All I can do is beg you, please spare my job to show that I can tread the straight and narrow and not get involved in a situation like this. I would not only ask. I beg you, please, don't destroy my life," Dahmer said.

"This enticing a child was the climax of my idiocy. It's just—it's going to destroy me, I'm afraid, this one incident. I don't know what in the world I was thinking when I did it. I know I was under the influence.''

Judge Gardner listened and considered. He even admitted that he faced a no-win situation with this man pleading before him.

The man in the black robe said that, unless Dahmer made fundamental changes in his behavior, ''you are going to repeat, because it's a drive. It's almost a biological urge that you have.''

Dahmer pleaded again. ''I can't stress it enough that I desperately want to change my conduct for the rest of my life.''

Gardner bought it. He gave Dahmer a chance. He ordered treatment for alcohol abuse and for his psychological problems, a therapy that didn't exist in prison.

''I could send you to prison and you wouldn't get any treatment for the problem. You'd come out probably worse than you are right now,'' Gardner said.

''This is the kind of thing that the prosecutor would just ask the judge to throw away the book, and the judge would say ten and ten [years] consecutive and good-bye. But if there is an opportunity to salvage you, I want to make use of that opportunity.''

Dahmer got five years for second-degree sexual assault, but Gardner stayed the sentence and ordered five years' probation. He was ordered to spend one year in the House of Correction, with work-release so that he could keep his nighttime job at the chocolate factory. He was also supposed to get psychological treatment.

Dahmer also got three years for enticing a child for immoral purposes. That sentence, too, was stayed.

In addition, Dahmer was ordered not to have any contact with anyone under eighteen. That meant he couldn't hang around schools, playgrounds, or parks.

But he didn't serve hard time.

No one from the Sinthasomphone family was in the courtroom to argue that this man should be sent to prison.

Judge William Gardner received a letter on December 10, 1989, from Jeffrey Dahmer inside the Community Correctional Center. In it, Dahmer asked for an early release, promising again to mend his ways.

"Sir," he wrote, "I have always believed that a man should be willing to assume responsibility for the mistakes that he makes in life. The world has enough misery in it without my adding more to it. Sir, I assure you that it will never happen again. This is why, Judge Gardner, I am requesting from you a sentence modification. So that I may be allowed to continue my life as a productive member of our society."

Dahmer was not a problem prisoner. He re-

ported back late once due to a communications mix-
up, and he lost two days of good time as a reprimand
for coming back drunk from a twelve-hour leave on
Thanksgiving. He was supposed to be back at 10
P.M. on the family holiday, but failed to show until
4:55 A.M. He was given a breath test when he got
back, apparently suffering from the holiday blues.

According to a report written by a corrections
officer, "Jeffrey claimed to have drunk a quart of
Jack Daniel's on Thanksgiving Day. It also appears
from a review of the presentence that Jeffrey is not
motivated toward any type of treatment. Essentially, that could be a problem area."

The whiskey binges were one of the reasons
Lionel Dahmer had qualms about his son's early
release. He argued against it, believing that Jeffrey
still needed to dry out and receive treatment for
alcoholism.

"I have tremendous reservations regarding
Jeff's chances when he hits the streets," Lionel
wrote to the judge. "Every incident, including the
most recent conviction for sex offense, has been
associated with and initiated by alcohol in Jeff's
case."

He sought strict alcohol treatment and follow-
up, and ended his letter with a plea of his own. "I
sincerely hope that you might intervene in some
way to help my son, who I love very much and for
whom I want a better life."

On March 2, 1990, Dahmer was free to go, after serving ten months.

Family members noticed he seemed hardened.

"Something happened to him in prison that he would never talk about," his stepmother, Shari Dahmer, told *The Plain Dealer*. "We all know what can happen to a child molester in prison. He had no light in his eyes. Jeff lost his soul in there. He said he'd never go back to prison."

Jeffrey Dahmer was back on the bar scene in the spring of 1990. He moved into the Oxford Apartments on May 13th.

The family of victim Raymond Smith, also known as Raymond Lamont and Ricky Beeks, said the man was last seen May 29.

The father of a ten-year-old daughter who lives in Rockford, Illinois, Smith had just come to Milwaukee to live with a half sister, Donita Grace. His family said he had a criminal record dating back to 1979 and had just gotten out of prison.

When he disappeared, no one reported it because the family said Smith often picked up and left for months at a time without notice. After he vanished this time, family members heard rumors that he had been shot.

Dahmer told police he met Smith at Club 219. Out of action for some time, Dahmer dusted off his old pickup lines. He invited Smith over to his new apartment to watch some videos. He sweetened the offer with money if Smith agreed to model for pictures.

Once inside the web, Smith was trapped. Dahmer gave him a drugged drink, then strangled him. Dahmer said he stripped the clothing from the dead man and performed oral sex on the corpse. Later, the body was cut up and the skull preserved. Dahmer painted it to make it look like a plastic model.

"The way he had to die was unreal. It was something out of a horror movie," said Grace.

Smith, a tenth-grade dropout, was raised by his grandmother in Rockford. He left behind two sisters, five half sisters, and one half brother.

"I don't blame Dahmer any more than I do the police department," said the grandmother, Thelma Smith, seventy-seven. "People had been calling them and they didn't investigate. You can't just lay it all on Dahmer. I believe he's sick, but if his probation officer had been keeping up on his case, maybe some of this could have been avoided. It was negligence on someone's part."

Regulars at the gay bars noted that a tall, thin man had stopped coming around. Nobody knew his real name; they just called him "The Sheik" because he always wore a turban or a headdress.

Lots of guys in the gay scene—hoping to protect their privacy and unwilling to come out of the closet—used pseudonyms, aliases, or just first names. Some people prefer not to know identities anyhow. A nod, a glance, the right body language and a perfect stranger could be lined up—all within a short amount of time.

Eddie Smith, twenty-eight, loved showing off his smooth face in front of a camera. At 6-foot-3 and 160 pounds, he wanted to be a professional model. With his flamboyance and Arab-style headdress, he was hard to miss at Club 219 and the other gay bars.

He was living with his sister, Carolyn, on the north side when he disappeared on June 14, 1990. He had vanished after a night of dancing at the local clubs and just before Milwaukee's Gay Pride event, which he planned to attend. She reported him missing on June 23. She said the police were very thorough in their concern up until the point when she told the investigating officer her brother was gay.

"His whole attitude changed. I really think that once he left, he tore up the report. The police later said the report was either lost or never filed," Carolyn said.

In March 1991, Carolyn Smith got a late-night phone call from a stranger.

"You don't have to bother looking for your brother," she said the voice told her.

"Why not?" she replied.

"Because he's dead," the voice said.

"How do you know?"

"Because I killed him."

Dahmer told police he picked up Smith at the Phoenix Bar, offering him money for sex and posing for pictures.

Smith took the stranger's bait. They took a cab for the twenty-three-block ride back to the Oxford Apartments on 25th Street, where Dahmer said they had oral sex. Dahmer then said he drugged Smith and strangled him, cutting up the body. He paused during his grisly chores to take four or five photographs.

But this time, Dahmer deviated from his normal procedure. Instead of saving the skull or other parts for his collection, Dahmer completely disposed of Smith's body by placing it in garbage bags and setting it out with the trash. He also said he later got rid of the pictures.

Dahmer identified Smith by photographs provided by his family.

Around this time, Dahmer had a close call with a fifteen-year-old boy living in a Hispanic foster home who was standing outside a gay bar.

The boy said Dahmer promised $200 if he would take his clothes off in front of the camera. The boy agreed, but he said Dahmer turned violent when he wanted to leave.

Dahmer smacked him in the back of the head

with a rubber mallet and tried to strangle him, but
the screaming boy promised he wouldn't call the
cops if he could go. Dahmer agreed and called a
taxi for him.

The boy knew him only as Jeffrey and police
were unable to follow up at the time, partly because
the boy wanted to hide his homosexuality from his
foster parents.

Dahmer's next two encounters had different
twists.

On September 2, 1990, Ernest Miller attended
services at the Golden Rule Church of God & Christ
in Milwaukee. That was the last his family saw of
him.

Born in Memphis, Tennessee, he moved with his
family to Milwaukee when he was an infant. An
accomplished dancer, he was a member of the Ko-
Thi Dance Company and was named best dancer as
a senior at Milwaukee High School of the Arts.

He lived with his grandmother in Chicago,
where he had a job as a busboy. He planned to
attend a dance school there in the fall.

Miller, twenty-four, was visiting relatives in Milwaukee over the Labor Day weekend when he met
Dahmer at a bookstore on 27th Street, just three
blocks from the Oxford Apartments. Dahmer offered money if Miller would come over.

Dahmer said they had sex, then he drugged

Miller and killed him, not by choking him, but by cutting his throat. After taking some pictures, Dahmer butchered the body and disposed of the flesh in acid, except for the biceps, which he wrapped and placed in the freezer.

He also kept the skull, which he boiled clean and then painted. And one more thing: he kept Miller's skeleton, which he bleached with acid.

"It's hard for us," said Stanley Miller, the man's uncle. "When we last saw Ernest, he was full of life, a very caring and loving person. And when we went to the coroner's office, there was nothing but a skeleton."

There were also peculiarities with David C. Thomas, last seen on September 24, 1990. But it had nothing to do with saving any mementos. Far from it.

Dahmer met Thomas downtown and invited him back home for a drink, and the two sat and chatted for a while. They didn't have sex, because, Dahmer told the police, the man wasn't his type.

However, Dahmer said he had already drugged Thomas and decided to kill him anyhow. Even though he didn't want sex, Dahmer figured the guy would be angry if he woke up after being drugged. He might even call the cops.

Dahmer cut up the body, stopping occasionally from his bloody toils to preserve the ritual on film.

But he threw away all the body parts, again, he said, because Thomas wasn't his type.

Leslie Thomas identified her brother by photographs of his severed head that were found in the apartment.

Thomas had a three-year-old daughter, Courtia. His girlfriend, Chandra Beanland, twenty-four, had reported him missing when he vanished. "Usually, he'd be gone for two or three weeks and then he'd call and come home," she said. "How can you tell a three-year-old her father's not coming back?"

Beanland's mother, Theedoris, challenged detectives when they came to break the news. "How can you tell us that there's nothing left? How can you tell us that was David?" she asked.

Then they showed her the picture.

There was nothing left but Dahmer's account of what happened. As in the cases of Tuomi, Doxtator, Guerrero, and Smith, the Thomas family had nothing to place beneath a headstone.

There was a period of about six months when Dahmer was quiet, from the end of 1990 to the beginning of 1991. Then, between March and July of 1991, eight people were killed, starting with Curtis Straughter.

Straughter, eighteen, was a handful for his grandmother.

"He was out all over with everybody. I'm an old

woman,'' said Katherine Straughter. He was last seen by friends in March.

Straughter, a high-school dropout, joined Gay Youth Milwaukee when he was fifteen, and he adopted the name Demetra. He yearned to be a model, to pose and smile and bat his eyelashes in front of the camera. But he recently lost his job as a nurse's aide, and he often needed money. Occasionally, he hit friends up for bus fare.

Dahmer offered Demetra money if he would pose for pictures. Dahmer told police he saw Straughter waiting for a bus near Marquette University, not far from the Oxford Apartments. He struck up a conversation, and Straughter was soon on his way back to this man's apartment.

Back at the Oxford Apartments, Straughter swallowed a drink laced with a sleeping potion. After he passed out, Dahmer removed his clothes and had oral sex with him. Then Dahmer said he wrapped a leather strap around Straughter's neck and squeezed the life out of him. As he hacked up the body, Dahmer paused to snap some pictures. They were the last frames taken of Curtis Straughter before his head was boiled and the skin removed to preserve his skull.

A medical examiner later matched the skull with Straughter's dental records.

* * *

The day the news broke on July 23, 1991, Mildred Lindsey and her family, heavy with dread, walked two blocks from their home to the Oxford Apartments. They had a sick feeling about what they would find.

Errol Lindsey, nineteen, was the youngest of Mildred's six children. He left home on April 7, 1991, to get a key made at a nearby shop—and disappeared without a trace. What can happen to you while you're getting a key made?

"It's like he just vanished from the world," Mrs. Lindsey said, hoping to get an answer and praying it would not be the wrong one.

Her sons, Michael and Reginald, passed out posters and pictures of Errol to media and police congregating at the Oxford Apartments, where the word sizzled on the streets that bodies had been discovered.

"We've been looking for a clue or a sign. When I heard about this, it was a heart-stopper. I got a bad feeling about it," Michael Lindsey told reporters.

"Errol is up there in that house, Mama." Yohanna Lindsey, Errol's sister, kept telling her mother.

As much as they didn't want to believe it, it was true.

Lindsey went to Dahmer's apartment for the lure of money. Dahmer said that once he got Lindsey inside, he drugged him and strangled him. After Errol was dead, Dahmer stripped off his clothes and had oral sex with the cadaver. He dismembered the body and kept the skull.

Lindsey was a drummer and a singer in the church choir. The Rev. Robert T. Wilson, pastor of the Christ Temple Baptist Church, called him "Cool Breeze" because of his refreshing personality.

Mildred plays piano and attends Bible classes at Greater Spring Hill Baptist Church. Now all she could do for her son was pray for his soul.

Everyone who knew Anthony Hughes seemed to like him. He had an incandescent smile and a gentle nature. He was deaf, a complication caused when he contracted pneumonia as an infant. He was also mute, but he communicated easily by sign language, reading lips, or if all else failed, writing notes. He was happy, outgoing, eager to make friends in his soundless world.

He loved to dance at Club 219. He couldn't hear the music, but he felt the reverberations of the driving bass chords and drums, and he never missed a beat.

Shirley Hughes had mothered three girls and three boys, and Tony was her youngest son. He lived in Madison, where he had moved because Milwaukee was becoming too dangerous. A neighbor in his old neighborhood had been killed, and the new city was much more tranquil. He had just gotten a new job at the United Plastic Co. His first two-week paycheck would be waiting for him when he got back to work, and he seemed happy with his $7-an-hour job.

Hughes, thirty-one, had come to visit his sister, Barbara, on May 24, a Friday night. Other family members were there. They laughed, looked at photo albums, and recalled good times.

He left about 10:30 P.M., the last time anyone in the family saw him, and headed for Club 219 to enjoy the music and the scene on the unofficial first weekend of summer.

Hughes had known Dahmer since October of 1989, when he met him at Club 219. His mother had seen the name "Jeff" written in her son's address book, but that's all she knew about him. Patrons at the bar said they last saw him with a tall white man who wore glasses.

Dahmer told police he wrote a note to Hughes with an offer: $50 if Hughes would come to his apartment, pose for photos, and watch videos. Hughes nodded yes.

Back inside No. 213, Dahmer offered a drink with a sleeping potion in it. When Hughes passed out, Dahmer said he killed him, dismembered the body, and kept his skull. Police identified him by matching dental records with a skull found July 22, but a sixth sense had already told Hughes's family that something awful had happened to him.

They had checked with everyone at Club 219. They distributed flyers with Tony's picture and description on it. They went to the Gay Pride festival for clues. They posted a reward. No luck, until police gave out the description of the man arrested after body parts were discovered in his apartment.

"After the description I heard, I knew deep inside my heart that my son would be one of the bodies found," said Mrs. Hughes, who teaches a Bible class at the Garden Homes Evangelical Lutheran Church.

"The way he died, it hurts. Words can't describe it. I prayed and asked the Lord to show me where my son was. I just wanted to know if he was dead or alive. Now I know."

The only time Mrs. Hughes saw Dahmer is on television, when he was brought into court stone-faced to be charged with murder.

"He didn't seem evil or anything. Just to look at him, you wouldn't think he could do the type of things they said he'd done," Mrs. Hughes said. "I don't have any hatred in my heart for anyone."

But anger burned deep inside friends who knew and loved Tony Hughes.

"For this guy to come into our lives and stalk and murder us, it's sickening. He has ruined and destroyed a lot of people's lives," said Larry Taylor

of the local gay group Black and White Men Together.

A service for Hughes was held July 30 at the
Garden Homes Evangelical Lutheran Church. A
family portrait adorned a casket draped with white
peonies and red roses. During the service, two
people deftly moved their fingers and hands in the
language of the deaf.

"There is a mountain of hurt in the Hughes
family right now. A mountain of hurt in our community and in this room right now," said the Rev.
Allen Sorum.

"Did Tony Hughes die in vain? If God does not
let a sparrow drop from the sky in vain, certainly
not your son, Mrs. Hughes. No, he did not die in
vain."

Just weeks before he was caught, Jeffrey Dahmer sat in Club 219, distantly sipping his drink. A
patron started talking about Anthony Hughes, saying what a shame it would be if something bad had
happened to such a nice guy.

He remembered Dahmer replying coldly, "He
got what he deserved."

Tony Hughes's body was still in the bedroom
when Dahmer left on May 26 to shop for men at the
Grand Avenue Mall. He was under court orders to
avoid anyone younger than eighteen, but he struck

up a quick conversation with a vulnerable Asian kid named Konerak Sinthasomphone.

Before dawn the next morning, after a close call when three cops had confronted Dahmer and even came to his apartment, the fourteen-year-old boy was among the victims.

It was a Sunday, in the middle of the three-day Memorial Day weekend, when the baby of the Sinthasomphone family headed toward the bus stop to play soccer with friends.

He played at Mitchell Park, several miles from his family's home on Milwaukee's north side in the 2600 block of N. 56th Street. He played every chance he got, dreaming so much of playing professional soccer that he had just started lifting weights to strengthen his maturing leg muscles. He wanted to go to college, to make something of himself.

A freshman at Pulaski High School, Konerak had a much easier time adapting to this new country than his parents, who were set in their Laotian ways. His English was superb. He liked what American kids liked: the Teenage Mutant Ninja Turtles, Tom & Jerry cartoons, swimming, climbing apple trees, fishing with his father in the dappled waters of Lake Michigan, flirting with girls.

He had the bounce of exuberant youth in his step when he left the house that day, wearing a white T-shirt and blue-jeans shorts. His family never saw him again.

Instead, Konerak wound up at the Grand Avenue Mall, where a lot of kids go to hang out. He had a bright, dimpled smile and stylish black hair accenting his Asian features. He caught the eye of Jeffrey Dahmer, who was under a judge's orders not to mix with children because of a sex offense involving a boy. That boy was Konerak's older brother, and now he was about to fall into the trap, despite warnings from his oldest brother that he should not talk to strangers.

In his statement to police, Dahmer said he enticed the boy to his apartment, where Sinthasomphone posed for a couple of pictures. Dahmer gave the boy a drink laced with a sleeping potion, and looked through his collection for a videotape. The drug knocked the boy out, so Dahmer used the opportunity to have oral sex with him.

Having run out of beer, Dahmer left the boy in the apartment and walked two blocks to a bar to get some more. In his absence, the boy apparently had recovered and wandered outside. Dahmer found him on the street, where citizens saw the naked boy staggering around, dazed, with blood on his legs. Nicole Childress ran to a nearby pay phone to call 911. Her cousin, Sandra Smith, went to help the boy, who she said was bleeding from his buttocks and was scraped and bruised.

What transpired next would rock the police department and rattle the city. Three officers were later suspended and two were dismissed, although no criminal charges were filed and the officers involved denied any wrongdoing. But some community groups said what transpired was indicative of police insensitivity to people of color and gays.

It was after midnight when Operator 71 took the call. The following conversations were transcribed from tapes released by police.

Childress: Hi. I'm on 25th and State, and there is this young man. He's butt-naked. He has been beaten up. He is very bruised up. He can't stand up. He has no clothes on. He is really hurt. I got no coat on. I just seen him. He needs some help.

Operator: Where—where is he?

Childress: 25th and State. At the corner of 25th and State.

Operator: He's just on the corner of the street?

Childress: Yeah, he's in the middle of the street. He fell out. We're trying to help him. Some people are trying to help him.

Operator: Okay. And he's unconscious right now?

Childress: They're getting him. He's bruised up. Somebody must have jumped on him and stripped him or whatever.

Operator: Okay. Let me put the fire department on the line. They'll send an ambulance. Just stay on the phone, okay?

Childress: Okay.

The fire department answered.

Childress: Can you send an ambulance to the corner of 25th and State?

Fire operator: What's the problem?

Childress: This butt-naked young boy, or man, or whatever. He's butt-naked. He's been beaten up real bad and he's fell out and people are trying to help him stand up. He can't stand up. He is butt-naked. He has no clothes on. He is very hurt.

Fire operator: Is he awake?

Childress: He ain't awake. They're trying to get him to walk. But he can't walk straight. He can't even see straight. Every time he stands up, he falls out.

Fire operator: 25th and State?

Childress: Yeah, a one way.

Fire operator: Okay.

Childress: Okay. Bye.

It was in the early hours of a holiday Monday when Patrolmen John A. Balcerzak, Joseph Gabrish, and Richard Porubcan were dispatched to the chaos outside the Oxford Apartments. They arrived a few minutes earlier than a unit of the fire department trained in emergency medicine. (Firefighters gave Konerak a blanket, but reports show they were told their services were no longer required.) A fourth officer, a trainee, was there, but did not take part in what followed.

Balcerzak, thirty-four, was a six-year veteran of the police force. He was one of three officers who won a merit citation for rescuing eight people from a burning building on August 24, 1989.

He also won a superior achievement award for helping to rescue a man trapped when heavy rains opened up a thirty-foot sinkhole on March 14, 1990. The commendation praised his "quick action and concerted effort."

Balcerzak had also made nineteen of what the police call "merit arrests," in which an officer has to go the extra mile to do his duty.

Gabrish, twenty-eight, had been a cop for seven years, after working two years as a police aide. There is heroism in his file jacket too.

He won a superior achievement award for helping to pull a man from a burning building on October 15, 1987. Six people perished in that fire, and the man Gabrish rescued had raced back into the smoke-filled building in a vain rescue attempt.

He is also credited with nineteen merit arrests.

Because of their experience and dedication, Balcerzak and Gabrish have worked as field-training officers for new recruits. They are volunteer mentors and get no extra pay for showing the ropes to younger officers.

Porubcan, twenty-five, was in the department for fifteen months, but he had already made his mark. He had five merit arrests and was known as a computer whiz. He helped the department develop a computer program to check pawn shops for stolen items.

Now it was time to sort out this scene on 25th Street.

In the two hours since coming on duty at midnight, Squad 36 had answered eight calls. There was a report of a man with a gun. On two separate occasions they responded to disputes between a man and a woman—the most mundane of police work. There was an injured-person report, a call to back up another squad at a shooting, gunshots being fired, a family in trouble. And a squad from a previous shift needed relief.

This next call would take sixteen minutes.

Sandra Smith, eighteen, was yelling at Dahmer not to hurt the boy, and she wheeled to fill the cops in on what was going on. She was startled by the answer.

"One of them told me, 'We'll handle this,' " Smith said later.

Dahmer started to reassure the police that they were witnessing only a domestic squabble—much to the chagrin of the black women, who sensed something was terribly amiss.

"We tried to give the policemen our names, but they just told us to butt out," Smith said. "One of them said to me, 'I've been investigating for seven years and I don't need an amateur telling me what to do.' "

Childress said she also tried to intervene.

"They was listening to Jeff. They wasn't listening to me. One of them told us to get lost or he'd take us downtown," Childress said. "If they had listened that night, that little boy would still be alive."

Dahmer, meanwhile, did some fast talking. He said there was nothing to worry about. His homosexual companion, who he called "Butch," had had too much to drink. They quarreled, and his partner ran out into the street. He'd even pulled this stunt before, Dahmer reassured the cops. Dahmer said the companion was nineteen, and he had an ID card to prove it. Now he just wanted to get him back inside quickly so everybody could get back to sleep.

Sinthasomphone, still under the influence of the drugs, was too incoherent to say anything to dispute that claim.

The police escorted Dahmer and the boy back to No. 213 to check out his story. Dahmer showed them Polaroids of the smiling companion posing in a bikini or bikini briefs, to back up the claim they were friends. Dahmer's story seemed to make sense, and nothing else in the apartment looked suspicious. Dahmer later told police that the body of Anthony Hughes, who he had killed three days before, was decaying in the bedroom.

The police radioed in.

Officer: Intoxicated Asian, naked male. [There was laughter on the tape, but it wasn't clear if it was coming from the car or the station.] Was returned to his sober boyfriend. [More laughter was heard on the tape.]

Police in the squad car said the assignment was completed. They were ready for more duties.

Officer: Ten-four. It'll be a minute. My partner is going to get deloused at the station. [More laughter was heard on the tape.]

There were five more calls that night before the shift ended.

If the cops were satisfied the job was finished, no one at the scene was. Glenda Cleveland, who is Sandra Smith's mother, wrote down the number of the squad car and decided to do some follow-up calling.

A data entry clerk and typesetter for C. P. Gauger Co., the thirty-seven-year-old Cleveland figured she was doing her duty as a responsible citizen and human being. She was doing what her parents taught their nine children to do—stand up for what's right.

She called the police again to find out what happened. The following conversations were recorded and released by police following an internal investigation.

Cleveland: A moment ago, ten minutes, my

Jeffrey Dahmer walks into Milwaukee County Court for his second appearance. (AP/WIDE WORLD PHOTOS)

Dahmer's 1977 Revere High School yearbook photo (AP/WIDE WORLD PHOTOS)

A Milwaukee police officer takes photos of bones found across an alley behind Dahmer's apartment building. (AP/WIDE WORLD PHOTOS)

Workers secure an outside doorway to Dahmer's apartment building. Apartment 213 is sealed off. (AP/WIDE WORLD PHOTOS)

Oliver Lacy of Chicago was named as the first confirmed victim in the killings. He is pictured here with his mother, Catharine. (AP/WIDE WORLD PHOTOS)

Ricky Beeks (*center in white cap*) was identified as one of the victims. (AP/WIDE WORLD PHOTOS)

Konerak Sinthasomphone, fourteen, disappeared in May 1989. He unsuccessfully tried to flee Dahmer's apartment and was later found killed and dismembered. Dahmer was convicted of sexually assaulting the boy's older brother in 1988. (AP/WIDE WORLD PHOTOS)

Members of the Sinthasomphone family sit on their front porch in Milwaukee following the identification of Konerak as a victim. (AP/WIDE WORLD PHOTOS)

Members of the Summit County Sheriff's department and Bath Township police videotape pieces of evidence found at Dahmer's former Bath, Ohio, residence and search for remains of Steven M. Hicks, allegedly the first person killed by Dahmer. (AP/WIDE WORLD PHOTOS)

Dahmer's attorney, Gerald Boyle, listens at a Milwaukee bond hearing. (AP/WIDE WORLD PHOTOS)

The Reverend Jesse Jackson escorts Shirley Hughes as he leads hundreds in a Milwaukee march in support of the families of victims. Hughes is the mother of victim Tony Hughes. (AP/WIDE WORLD PHOTOS)

Hundreds of people gather at Milwaukee's MacArthur Square as they hold a candlelight vigil in remembrance of the victims. (AP/WIDE WORLD PHOTOS)

Dahmer at his first court appearance (AP/ WIDE WORLD PHOTOS)

daughter and my niece flagged down a policeman when they walked up on a young child being molested by a male guy. And no information or anything was being taken . . . I was wondering . . . I mean I'm sure further information must be needed. The boy was naked and bleeding.

She was transferred to another officer.

Officer: Hello, this is . . . the Milwaukee police.

Cleveland: Yes, there was a squad car that was flagged down earlier this evening, about fifteen minutes ago.

Officer: That was me.

Cleveland: Yeah, uh, what happened? I mean, my daughter and niece witnessed what was going on. Was there anything done about the situation? Do you need their names, or information or anything from them?

Officer: No, not at all.

Cleveland: You don't?

Officer: Nope. It's an intoxicated boyfriend of another boyfriend.

Cleveland: Well, how old was this child?

Officer: It wasn't a child. It was an adult.

Cleveland: Are you sure?

Officer: Yup.

Cleveland: Are you positive? Because this child doesn't even speak English. My daughter had, you know, dealt with him before and seen him on the street catching earthworms.

. . . .

Officer: Ma'am. Ma'am. Like I explained to you, it is all taken care of. It's as positive as I can be. . . ? I can't do anything about anybody's sexual preferences in life.

Cleveland: Well, no, I'm not saying anything about that, but it appeared to have been a child. This is my concern.

Officer: No, no, he's not.

Cleveland: He's not a child?

Officer: No, he's not. Okay? And that's a boy-friend–boyfriend thing. And he's got belongings at the house where he came from. . . .

Cleveland: Oh, I see.

Officer: Okay?

Cleveland: Okay, well I am just, you know, it appeared to have been a child. That was my concern.

Officer: I understand. No, he is not. Nope.

Cleveland: Okay. Okay. Thank you. Bye.

The officers had taken Dahmer's name and other information. But according to a subsequent internal police investigation, when they got back to the station they failed to write a formal report. They also failed to run Dahmer's name through the crime computer, which would have spit out the fact he had a criminal record for a sexual assault and was still on probation.

Glenda Cleveland, her daughter, and her niece

still weren't satisfied. They sensed something the police didn't, and it haunted them for weeks.

"I can't believe that the police couldn't see something was very wrong," Cleveland said. "Somebody goofed along the line. I think [the police] just took the whole situation and left it at that. . . . There's nothing funny about a boy bleeding and hurt and drugged."

Their only possible conclusion was that because they were black and the boy was Asian, the white policemen believed the story of a white Jeffrey Dahmer.

It wasn't the last time she called police.

When she read a story about a missing Laotian boy named Konerak Sinthasomphone, Cleveland called to talk about the May 27 encounter.

"They said they would have someone come out and talk to me and take the information. And no one ever came," she said.

C. Nicol Padway, chairman of the Fire and Police Commission, which oversees the police department, later praised Cleveland as an example to be followed.

"She was not content to sit by idly and merely watch, but rather she persisted in her efforts to assist another human being," Padway said.

Dahmer apparently didn't give it much thought. After the police left, he turned his attention back to his fourteen-year-old prey. Dahmer said he strangled him and then had oral sex with him. He took more pictures for his collection before dismembering the body.

Konerak Sinthasomphone's skull was among those found July 23 in the apartment. Authorities identified him by matching the skull to his dental records. Four others died after him.

There would be much more said by and about the police later on.

The news made no sense to the Laotian family. No, it just couldn't be. Police had come to their door to show them pictures of their youngest child, found in the apartment of a man admitting to seventeen murders. Yes, it was Konerak. But it just couldn't be. Especially since Jeffrey Dahmer was the same man who had molested a son in 1988.

"The whole thing is crazy. It is terrible," said Anoukone Sinthasomphone, twenty-seven, the oldest sibling. "I don't know what to say."

What could anyone say? They had fled a hard life for the promise of America. Now . . .

"I escaped the communists and now this happens. Why?" the father muttered to a relative.

At fifty-two, he is unemployed, struggling to adapt to this new life, supported in part by his sons and daughters, who had found work and purpose in Milwaukee's factories. From the kitchen of his white, well-kept bungalow, he was unable to talk about what happened. At the funeral services, he sat bleary-eyed, his face graven with disbelief. He clutched a white hanky for the well of tears.

His wife, Somdy, fifty, had fits of uncontrollable shaking and was hospitalized for three days after feeling faint.

The family was numb with shock, unable to speak, unable to eat, unable to grasp a pain that renders everything in life meaningless.

Their grief was ministered to by the Rev. Peter Burns, a Catholic priest from Sheboygan, who has known the family almost since the day they arrived in the area. He could only try to guess at the depth of the mourning.

"They left Laos to come to a country where they would be free and where there would be peace, and it was a torturous journey, from what I'm told," Father Burns said.

"Obviously, anyone who has gone through such a tragedy as this would wonder if they've chosen the right path for their lives. The family is filled with a lot of different emotion. Anger is one of them."

Experts who are supposed to help console survivors of tragedies were also left speechless.

"I can't think of anything worse. I absolutely can't fathom the tragedy of it," said Jo Kolanda, coordinator of Milwaukee County's victim-witness program.

Under Buddhist custom, families set out food

for a deceased member until a final ceremony puts the soul to rest. It's a Laotian form of a wake, and it usually lasts two or three days. This one dragged on for two weeks until the police released Konerak's remains, which the family had cremated.

Somdy Sinthasomphone removed all the photographs of her youngest son, except an eight-by-ten color portrait placed on a cloth-covered coffee table. It was flanked by two white votive candles burning in a clear glass container. Behind it was a flower. Set before the picture, taken when Konerak was in the eighth grade, was a glass of orange juice. And in bowls decorated with oriental patterns were Konerak's favorite snack of sliced apples and spiced sauce, and traditional Laotian dishes with beef, pork, and rice.

A card taped above the hand-tended memorial read: *Earth hath no sorrow that heaven cannot heal.*

Father Burns said that the boy loved life. "He was, like all teenagers, full of energy, full of joy, of many hopes and dreams. He will certainly be missed. . . . The ending of such a young life causes great pain."

His family had called police the day after Konerak disappeared. They searched everywhere they could imagine—even in other states. They never even thought that Dahmer might be connected to their pain again. Police said there was no motive of revenge on Dahmer's part, such as getting back at the boy who sent him to prison by killing his brother. Dahmer said from jail he didn't know the boy he had molested and the boy he killed were related.

Anoukone Sinthasomphone, the family spokesman, said the family had been reassured by police in 1988 that Dahmer would be locked up for a long time for the evil he did back then.

"We never thought he was going to be out," the brother said.

Someone had called the family three days after Konerak disappeared and said in a deep voice, "Konerak is in danger right now." No one knows for sure if it was Dahmer or not.

Corinne Giesa, a neighbor, was outraged that the boy who she used to see racing his brother home from school had been murdered. "It makes me very angry," she told reporters. "Too many boys have been sacrificed since May, when police had a chance to stop it."

Outrage was in plentiful supply in Milwaukee neighborhoods.

On August 1, a candlelight vigil was held downtown at Zeidler Park. About 150 members of the Asian community had gathered, seeking a release for the roiling emotions in their hearts.

Shoua Nao Xiong spoke for many when he claimed police had a tendency of "looking the other way'' if Asians were in trouble. They expected such cold indifference in the war-torn lands they left. They didn't expect to find this in America.

"I have seen this type of looking the other way, this odd kind of quietness, many times before," said Xiong, executive director of Milwaukee's Lao Family Community Center, Inc.

"When we came here, we came to live without fear, but we find that decent people of all races are living in fear here. Living here is becoming more like living in a jungle war zone.

"We are finding that there are gaps in the system for some of us. Is there nothing we can trust to protect us here?"

In other areas of the city, blacks and gays were asking the same questions.

About 150 people came to pay their final respects to Konerak on August 8. The Becker-Ritter Funeral Home on Lisbon Avenue was scented with the fragrance of fresh-cut flowers but heavy with the air of grief. Mourners viewed a closed casket concealing the final remains, which police had found in a dingy apartment.

Family and friends were there. So were total strangers, mothers with kids of their own, trying to comprehend an unbearable sorrow and praying that something like this would never happen to one of their children.

People the family never heard of sent sympathy

cards or delivered cookies and baked goods to the house.

A traditional Laotian service was held the next day; a Catholic funeral was offered August 12.

The family, though shaken, hadn't given up on the ideals their new homeland is supposed to stand for. They didn't file any lawsuits or demand police resignations in the wake of what happened. "Everybody's angry. Not only us. The whole city. The whole world is angry. We have to take care of the family, try to calm everybody down and try to accept what happened and what's going on," Anoukone Sinthasomphone said. "I trust in American law. I trust in America."

Fate wasn't finished with the family just yet.

Friends and well-wishers had donated $6,000—crumpled bills dug from their pockets and wallets—to give to the family. It was a gesture of sympathy, some small way of helping a family out in a time of need, something Midwesterners do without being asked.

At least the family had some cash to pay for memorial services and funeral costs, costs that had wiped out the savings of Anoukone Sinthasomphone, a welder.

But sometime late Sunday or early Monday, just before the funeral, the money was stolen during a burglary at the home of one of the boy's relatives. It had been inside a wallet that was in a purse. The purse, minus the wallet with the money, was found in a nearby trash can the next day.

Sometimes, when the workers on the graveyard shift at the Ambrosia Chocolate Co. asked Dahmer how his weekend went, he told them about the party scene in Chicago. One time, he spent $100 on a cab ride for the ninety-mile trip, which seemed a bit extravagant since he was always complaining he was strapped for cash.

Dahmer liked the action in Chicago. He also liked it because nobody knew him. Milwaukee had eight gay bars, with the same old crowd all the time. The bigger city to the south had about 76 spots. He was anonymous. He could go to any one of the hangouts on Halsted Street—such as The Manhole Club or Roscoe's—without being noticed.

Chicago also offered a freewheeling Gay Pride parade. Chicago's version isn't as flashy as the march in San Francisco, which features female motorcyclists who call themselves "Dykes on Bikes" and men who dress in nun's habits, webbed stockings, and spiked heels—the Sisters of Perpetual Indulgence led by Sister Vicious Power-Hungry Bitch. It's also not as wild as the parade in New York, where men in drag, lingerie, and spiked heels strut down Fifth Avenue. They dance, blow kisses, and distribute condoms.

But the Chicago parade offers a chance to come

out of the closet, at least for an afternoon, with thousands of others. It's a chance to laugh and frolick while calling attention to serious issues such as AIDS research and homophobia.

Dahmer was in Chicago for that Sunday celebration on June 30, standing in the crowd, watching the gays and lesbians march, checking out the scene. He also had a minor misfortune. He filed a report with the Chicago police saying his wallet had been lost or stolen.

At the bus station, he met Matthew Turner, twenty, an aspiring model who loved to cruise the clubs and sing in the lip-synching contests. He had a stage name, Donald Montrell.

Turner had run away from his home in Flint, Michigan, in 1990, and found himself at the Teen Living Program, a halfway house for runaways on Chicago's North Side. He stayed for two months before leaving the prior Christmas. Currently, he worked at the Chicago Style Pizza & Eatery.

Dahmer made an advance that hooked Turner: he'd give him money if he would come back to Milwaukee and pose nude for photographs and watch some videos. It must have been an attractive offer, because he had to take a Greyhound bus with Dahmer for the ninety-mile trip to Milwaukee, then switch to a City Vet cab for a ride to the one-bedroom flat on 25th Street.

Dahmer slipped him a drink spiked with drugs.

When Turner dozed off, Dahmer said he tightened a leather strap around Turner's neck until he was dead. He cut off the man's head and wrapped it in a plastic bag. The bag was secured with a fastener, then deposited in the freezer. He put the torso in a blue fifty-seven-gallon barrel with a black plastic lid.

Later, the awful news staggered Rosa Fletcher, who had lost her only child. "You always thought about something happening to other people's kids, but you never think about it until it happens to your own child, your only child," Fletcher told a television interviewer.

The family has filed a $4.5 million suit against the Milwaukee Police Department, claiming their son might still be alive if they had stopped Dahmer on May 27 when he was with Konerak Sinthasomphone.

"If this could be a form of vindication for Matt, we're all for it," said Wadell Fletcher, Turner's stepfather. "We're left empty, with nothing."

The Fletchers' lawyer, Charles W. Giesen of Madison, Wisconsin, said the case involved negligence. "It was more than a simple, honest mistake. It went beyond that," Giesen said. "One of the purposes of filing the claim is to maybe shock or jolt them into hopefully preventing another tragedy like this from happening."

There was no immediate comment from the city.

* * *

It was Friday night, July 5, the start of the weekend following a gala Fourth of July. Jeremiah Weinberger was looking for his own brand of fireworks at one of Chicago's gay dance spots, Carol's Speakeasy. Crowds gather there on Wells Street in the Old Town neighborhood every weekend to watch the male strippers and other attractions.

Weinberger, twenty-three, struck up a conversation with a six-foot-tall blond man, who appeared to be about thirty. The stranger made a suggestion. Why not come back to Milwaukee for a good time?

Weinberger mulled it over. He sought advice from Ted Jones, a former roommate who worked with Weinberger for a distributor of gay and lesbian adult videos.

"Well, should I go with this guy?" Weinberger said.

Jones, thirty-eight, checked him out.

"He seems all right," Jones said he told his friend.

A month later, a stunned Jones recalled the events. "Who's to say what a serial killer looks like?"

Weinberger gave the stranger a nod over the pulsing beat of the dance music. Nobody ever saw him again in Chicago.

They caught a Greyhound north to Milwaukee,

then took a City Vet cab back to 25th Street, where they had sex. Dahmer said that Weinberger stayed over, but expressed a desire to leave on the second day.

Dahmer didn't want to be left alone, so he fed Weinberger a drink with a sleeping potion in it. He strangled him with his hands. Then out came the camera and the cutting tools.

After dismembering the body, Dahmer stopped to take more pictures. He wrapped Weinberger's head in a plastic bag, fastened it with a twist, and placed it in his freezer with Turner's frozen head. The body was dumped in the fifty-seven-gallon drum, also joining what was left of Turner.

After his arrest, Dahmer told police he couldn't stand the thought of being abandoned, and he insisted that his companions stay, even if it meant slaying them.

"He killed them so they wouldn't leave. He didn't do it just for the hell of it. The experience of his childhood probably had a lot to do with it," said a Milwaukee police investigator who questioned Dahmer in jail.

When Weinberger failed to return, the grapevine twitched with word that men were missing. Friends printed posters with Weinberger's picture and description, asking anyone with information to call. A missing person notice ran in two gay publications, the *Windy City Times* and *Gay Chicago*.

There were rumors a killer was stalking the bars, and a warning went up about "stranger danger"— going off with someone you didn't know.

Even though Weinberger's friend and relatives feared something was terribly wrong, the news about what was found in No. 213 in Milwaukee hit hard.

"He wasn't the type of person who would fly off on a whirlwind vacation. We never dreamed we'd find him like this," said Tim Gideon, Weinberger's former roommate.

"My son was hypnotized by a cobra. Unfortunately, he was bit," said David Weinberger.

The youngest of Catherine Lacy's three sons had been missing for a week. She was frantic. So when she heard on the news that a man in handcuffs had escaped from a nearby apartment, she, too, headed for the throng assembling on 25th Street.

"Maybe this was my son that got loose," Catherine Lacy remembered thinking.

No such luck. It was another man.

But before the day was out, she learned that her baby, twenty-three-year-old Oliver Lacy, was the first victim to be positively identified. Lacy, the father of a two-year-old son, had moved to Milwaukee four months earlier to be with his child and fiancée, Rose Colon.

Police found his severed head in the refrigerator.

His identification card was also found in the apartment. Mrs. Lacy had to identify a picture of her son's lifeless face. "I wanted to find out. I wanted to see for myself. I had to see for myself," Mrs. Lacy said.

Weeks later, she went back to the Oxford Apartments to the door marked No. 213. It was padlocked by police and had a sign tacked to it warning people to stay clear. People in the building saw her place her hand on the wood grain and weep for her son.

Oliver Lacy had worked at Pioneer Commercial Cleaning, a janitorial and cleaning service. He was originally from Oak Park, Illinois, and was on the track team at Oak Park–River Forest High School.

On Monday, July 15, Lacy went for ice cream at the Grand Avenue Mall downtown. When he failed to return by the next day, Mrs. Lacy alerted police.

"I felt something was wrong, because my son would call me," she said.

Dahmer said he met Lacy on 27th Street, just two blocks from home. Lacy said he was going to a cousin's house, but Dahmer made a better proposition. Why not come over to model for pictures?

Dahmer said they removed their clothes and gave each other body rubs. He said he gave Lacy a drink that knocked him out, and then he strangled him. After Lacy was dead, Dahmer said, he sodomized the corpse.

He cut up the body, placing Lacy's head in a

box in the refrigerator next to the open box of Arm & Hammer baking soda.

He also told police he kept the man's heart in the freezer compartment "to eat later." Other parts were placed in the freezer also.

"I don't know how this person lured my son," Mrs. Lacy said.

The last time anyone saw Joseph Bradehoft was July 19. He left an apartment rented in the name of his brother, Donald, for a job interview.

He was visiting Milwaukee and looking for work, and planned to move his wife and two small children from St. Paul, Minnesota.

Dahmer was riding a bus when he spotted Bradehoft carrying a six-pack of beer and standing at a bus stop near Marquette University. Dahmer said he got off and approached the man, asking him if he'd take money for coming over his apartment to pose for pictures and watch some porn tapes.

Bradehoft agreed. Inside the apartment, Dahmer said, they had oral sex. Then, Dahmer said, he drugged the man, and while he was asleep, brought out the leather strap he used to choke the others.

He butchered the body, placing the head inside a plastic bag and tucking it into the freezer with the heads of Turner and Weinberger. The body was placed in the fifty-seven-gallon barrel in the bedroom.

Bradehoft's indentification card was found inside the apartment.

"He was a person who had no trouble striking up a conversation, and Joe would have no hesitation in going with someone," said Mary Roy, a former acquaintance from Greenville, Illinois. "He was very trusting."

Bradehoft was the last of Dahmer's victims, before the escaped Tray Edwards would bring the whole house of horrors crashing down.

7

Portrait of a Killer

It seems unimaginable that there are people who kill, and kill, and kill again because they enjoy it. Part of the thrill is being sexually excited during and after a murder. The drive is so powerful that if killers aren't actually doing it, they're thinking about past deeds or fantasizing about the next time. And those who do unspeakable things seem frightening close to normal.

Serial killers are the subject of endless fascination. Their numbers range from about three dozen documented cases to estimates into the hundreds. But experts agree it appears to be a growing phenomenon.

The behavioral sciences unit at the FBI Academy in Quantico, Virginia, began studying serial killers in the 1970s to try to identify them rather than explain them. However, the information provided clues on what drives them.

One report on sexual serial killers was done by Robert K. Ressler and John E. Douglas of the FBI Academy, with the help of those who study the human mind. None of the characteristics they found applied in all instances, but there were patterns noted in a study group of thirty-six serial killers.

Almost all were white males, usually the oldest child, in a home with a stable source of income that provided a self-sufficient economic level. They were smart and shrewd, yet they were underachievers, content to slide by in their studies or jobs.

They were loners, neither nurtured nor protected by parents too absorbed in their own problems to pay attention.

Most shared a common link to physical, psychological, or sexual abuse incurred as a child, but neglect may also take the subtle form of bickering parents too busy arguing to heed their children's cries. They do not bond with a parent and come across as aloof, self-centered loners. Parents, those voices of authority, have no influence over behavior. Nobody can say no, and there is no inner voice or conscience that tells them to stop.

Although most start out in a two-parent home,

problems were noted in the mother or father's background: alcohol or drug abuse; criminal, psychiatric, or sexual problems. In 43 percent of the cases, at least one parent was absent at some time before the subject reached the age of eighteen.

Cruelty to animals was a common trait. It was noted in 46 percent of the adolescents and 36 percent of the adults. So the behavior doesn't change, just the objects. Some psychiatrists theorize that they pick on animals to vent anger felt toward people.

Because serial killers are left alone in their own worlds, their fantasies substitute for human behavior. In a sense, dreams become reality.

Other common behavioral traits include compulsive masturbation, isolation, chronic lying, rebelliousness, fire setting, stealing, cruelty to children, poor body image, and phobias.

The FBI profile lists the essential feature behind a serial killer's behavior as a means "to achieve sexual excitement."

"Fantasy becomes the primary source of emotional arousal, and that emotion is a confused mixture of sex and aggression," the report says.

Themes include dominance, revenge, violence, rape, molestation, power, control, torture, mutilation, and inflicting pain.

If the cruelty is not stopped, emerging serial

killers find their way to future abuses. It is as if they are guided to a sinister destiny.

"First, the early violent acts are reinforced, as the murderers are either able to express rage without experiencing negative consequences or are impassive to any prohibitions against these actions.

"Second, impulsive and erratic behavior discourages friendships. The men either as children or adolescents feel estranged from people. Either by daydreaming or fantasies, they become absorbed in their own thoughts," the report said.

Studies of Dahmer's particular motives are just beginning. They may be debated for years. But initially, he seems to fit a subcategory the professionals call borderline—a personality that makes him prone to murderous rage if he thinks he is being abandoned, and a perversion for having sex with victims after they are dead.

"The borderline personality disorder is marked by a fear of abandonment and the inability to tolerate isolation or boredom. One current theory is that it may be related to childhood abuse," said Dr. Park Dietz, a forensic psychiatrist from Newport Beach, California, who served as a consultant to the FBI on the serial killer study. "People who fear abandonment can become outraged when someone they want to stay is about to leave.

"The ordinary serial killer gets to be that way by being antisocial or otherwise character-flawed and also by being sexually deviated, usually sadistic and necrophilic," Dietz said.

Sexually sadistic serial killers have no conscience. They are unmoved by suffering in others. They are controlled, calculating, cunning. They may take photographs or keep a journal of their deeds. They keep souvenirs or trophies, usually a piece of jewelry or a piece of underwear, but sometimes a body part, such as a skull, a penis, a patch of skin. The trophies are fond reminders of memorable occasions, as pleasing to the perverted as photographs from a beach vacation, or an autographed baseball would be to others. Body parts take on the value of mementos of conquest. Like a centerfold, they can also be a future turn-on for masturbating.

Victims are depersonalized and treated as things, not human beings. They are perceived with all the feeling given an inflatable doll, so anything goes—even using them for sex after they are dead.

"These were sexual props, not people. They have no more meaning than a dildo," Dietz said.

Sexual killers prefer to strangle their victims. Of 130 people killed by a group of serial killers that Dietz studied, 58.4 percent were strangled—by ropes, cords, belts, or bare hands. There is a sense of power and dominance as the last breath is squeezed from the body, he said.

"It's a very personal, intimate means. One can

actually feel the victims expire, see them go into convulsions and hear their last efforts to breathe. It's not messy. And most surprising perhaps, it allows for the possibility to resuscitate them and do it again, sort of an instant replay," Dietz said.

Dismemberment is sometimes a way to hide the deed or dispose of the body, but it takes an awful lot of work to get rid of, say, 160 pounds of human remains. Cannibalism is rare; when it occurs, it's usually related to consuming an empowering part like the heart.

Such evil is spellbinding even if it is revolting.

"We're fascinated by it. We turn these guys into celebrities," said James Fox, a criminologist at Northeastern University in Boston.

"No screen, no test, allows us to predict these guys ahead of time. If Jeffrey Dahmer looked bizarre, if he looked crazy, if he drooled or wet himself, no one would get close to him. On the surface, he blends in. That's what makes him so dangerous. He has no stop mechanism—no conscience, no remorse, no capacity for empathy. His sexual fantasies are fused with hatred. He can't stop the fact he's aroused, but he's angry at being aroused. You can see the twisted logic."

Dr. David Silber, a psychologist at George Washington University, also noted that a killer may seem remarkably unremarkable—at least on the surface.

"If there's anything monstrous about him, it's the monstrous lack of connection to all things we think of as being human—guilt, remorse, worry, feelings that would stop him from hurting, killing, torturing," Silber said. "What went on in his mind is a secret known only to him and may never be known."

In the book *Mass Murder: America's Growing Menace,* coauthors James Fox and Jack Levin wrote, "The pleasure and exhilaration that the serial killer derives from repeated murder stems from absolute control over other human beings.

"Serial killers almost without exception choose vulnerable victims—those who are easy to dominate," according to the authors. "The serial killer typically picks on innocent strangers who may just be accessible."

Psychiatrist Helen Morrison, who spent hundreds of hours studying serial killer John Wayne Gacy, believes that victims of serial killers are symbols of someone or something significant in a murderer's life, she said.

She also theorizes that the killer has some type of nonverbal communication with the victim, and there is something significant about the way they look.

"There's something unique in that interaction," she told the *Los Angeles Times*. "If you take photos, or physical descriptions, of the victims, what will strike you is the similarity in look.''

So what went wrong with Jeffrey Dahmer? Experts will be sifting through the rubble of a thirty-one-year-old life in ruins for clues, but some opinions are being proposed.

Dr. Ashok Bedi, clinical director of the Milwaukee Psychiatric Hospital, has not spoken to, or examined, Dahmer. But from what he has studied about the case, he feels there is a recurring theme— fear of being deserted.

"I think the big fear he has is one of being abandoned. He is a man lost, without a soul, without a sense of connectedness to the world around him," Bedi said.

Feelings of neglect emerged in childhood, which became a sort of emotional abandonment, Bedi said. The family failed to provide him a foundation, an infrastructure that would support him. Then came the untidy events leading up to a divorce: a distant father who moved into his own space and eventually out of the house; a mother who took his younger brother away and left him all alone.

A lot of kids who don't get the attention they crave at home seek it at school. Dahmer did with his clownish antics, but he wound up getting erased from a picture in which he didn't belong. More abandonment, Bedi said.

"He was shunned and humiliated and essentially

blotted out. It must have left him with a terrible sense of disintegration of self. He felt the way he made his later victims feel. He dismembered them and blotted them out too. He projected his feelings on his victims. He didn't want to be blotted out again," Bedi said.

After failing in college, Dahmer joined the army, where many people seek camaraderie and fellowship in what can be an extended family, with its discipline and authority figures and brothers in arms. Dahmer was discharged from this family, too, mainly due to his own affliction with the bottle.

"He kept giving off signals. He fell through every crack he could fall through," Bedi said.

The psychiatrist also theorized that there was a twisted fusion of anger and sexual drives within Dahmer.

"He showed a lot of confusion between sexuality and aggression. People who are regressed have very little capacity to distinguish between the two. So when they are feeling sexual toward someone, they will show it by aggression. That would include mutilating the victims, cannibalism, making love to the corpse, defiling the body," Bedi said.

One of the most significant events in Dahmer's life came in March 1991, when his mother called him after five years of no contact, Bedi said. The reunion came in a phone call from California, which was noted by Dahmer's probation officer, Donna Chester.

"Subject said conversation went well. She knows he is gay and has no problems accepting it. Subject says they will maintain their contact," Chester wrote.

Seven people were killed in Dahmer's apartment between March and July 19, 1991—something that Bedi called a "killing frenzy." He theorized that Dahmer was afraid that once contact was made anew with his mother, she would abandon him yet again.

"I think it was a very significant event in the crime spree. My hypothesis is, she is barely reconnected. There is tentative acceptance of his being gay. But he thinks, if history repeats itself, he'll soon be abandoned again. There must be something unresolved here. This must have been extremely painful," Bedi said.

"I think he got caught because he wanted to get caught. It was his way of avoiding the massive abandonment he felt. He wanted to get caught before his mother changed her mind and abandoned him again. It came at a very high price to society and himself. This is not to explain his behavior, but to understand it."

Scraps of information about Dahmer are contained in probation officer Donna Chester's eighty-one-page file. There is no conclusive portrait to be drawn from reports, only snippets and clues that remain part of a much larger puzzle.

Portions of the report distributed to the media are blotted out to exclude confidential information. Her written notes hint of a life unraveling. Dahmer sometimes showed up for his visits looking disheveled and unkempt. He spoke of alienation from his family, his problems understanding his homosexuality, his drinking, his deep-seated anger, his problems at work leading up to his dismissal. He spoke several times of suicide, telling Chester on one occasion that the only solution to his problems was "to jump off a tall building."

Under Wisconsin law, a probation officer is supposed to visit an offender every thirty days. But in Dahmer's case, Chester had the consent of a supervisor to waive those requirements. The reason: Her caseload was too full, and his neighborhood was so bad that she didn't want to visit alone. There weren't any spare probation officers to go with her.

Dahmer's last visit to Chester's office was July 18, the day before, according to what he told police, he killed his final victim and three days after he had killed Oliver Lacy. Having just lost his job, Dahmer's life was crashing down around him.

"The client has dirty clothes, is unshaven and during the interview was yawning as if having problems staying awake," Chester noted.

"The client is in severe financial difficulty. He will lose his apartment on the 1st of August. He talks again of suicide."

At their last meeting, Chester arranged for Dahmer to seek immediate psychiatric help. She gave him a list of food banks and places where he could get free meals. She gave him advice on getting a new job. And she arranged to have him placed on a Salvation Army housing list to cope with his pending eviction for being unable to pay his $296 a month rent at the Oxford Apartments.

The portions of Dahmer's file detailing the psychological and mental-health counseling he received are protected by state law from being made public.

But Dahmer received care throughout the time he was on probation, according to Roger Miller, assistant regional director for Wisconsin's probation and parole services.

"His file is replete with him presenting himself as depressed. He had psychological counseling from day one," Miller said.

Dahmer's first contact with the probation office was March 29, 1990, four weeks after he was released from jail. His first act was to sign a series of rules, some typed as part of the standard form.

"You shall make every effort to accept the opportunities and counseling offered by the supervision," one of the fourteen rules said.

"You shall avoid all contact which is in violation

of statute ordinances, or which is not in the best interest of the public welfare or your rehabilitation," said another.

His caseworker, Donna Chester, was a rookie probation officer assigned to the sex-offenders unit of the division of probation and parole. She started her job three months earlier.

She thought she was counseling a man who had sexually assaulted a boy. She had no idea he had killed and would kill throughout her contact with him.

In a section adding rules imposed by the agent, Chester listed her handwritten demands:

"You shall have no unsupervised contact with any person under the age of eighteen years without prior agent approval," she wrote.

"You shall consume no alcohol whatsoever."

She might have just as well asked him to be taller.

On Dahmer's first visit to her office, on April 12, Chester noted that she felt the client needed to identify his sexual feelings. She told him to start thinking about who he was and what would make him happy in life. She wrote that Dahmer was receptive about discussing his sexuality. But she also wrote that he admitted to drinking alone, and that that was when his behavior changed and problems arose. She told him to learn how to deal with his problems with alcohol first, "and then we will begin to discuss sexual tendencies."

During a visit on April 27, Dahmer told Chester he would be more comfortable talking about his sexual orientation now that he knew he was not being judged for it. He also explained he had no friends and had isolated himself from society. Chester also noted Dahmer seemed very depressed. She thought he had been unable to find a decent apartment on the $8.75-an-hour salary (he had gotten a raise from $8.25) he earned at Ambrosia Chocolate Co. Chester wrote that she told him "to check out stores for used furniture . . . and buy one item a week for the house."

She also wrote, "Subject seems to give up easily. Subject does not want to solve his own problems. Looks for others to help him."

There was also a reference to a telephone conversation with Lionel Dahmer on April 27. He said he wanted to help his son as much as possible. "Father stated subject had been abused by a neighbor at the age of eight. May be reason why subject has problems with sexuality issues. Told father would notify him if something came up," Chester wrote. Lionel Dahmer has since denied saying this to the probation officer and Jeffrey Dahmer later denied to the police that he had ever been abused.

Notes are brief on the May 15 visit. The only

insight is Dahmer's desire to check out a career in
real estate.

A week later, Dahmer paid her an unannounced
visit. He said he had accidentally missed one of his
counseling sessions required by the terms of his
probation. Dahmer came to see her because he
didn't know what would happen. She called the
counselor to reschedule, but wasn't sure if there
was an opening. "Subject stated he could be in
serious trouble if he does not comply with the
treatment program," she wrote. Then she sent him
home to wait for her phone call.

On his regularly scheduled visit, on May 29, a
different Jeffrey Dahmer came to Chester's office.

"Subject looked bad today. Usually has a neat
appearance, but was unkempt and unshaven today," Chester wrote. Dahmer explained that his
apartment had been robbed, but police had no record of a break-in. Dahmer later purchased a sophis-
ticated security system that went off whenever the
door was so much as bumped. Chester wrote down
the advice she gave her client: "Told subject there
really is nothing he can do about it except learn
from his mistake and try to find a better area to live
in." (The family of Raymond Lamont Smith said he
disappeared on May 29. That date conflicts with the
one Dahmer gave police on his meeting with Smith.
He said they had an encounter about two months

after he moved into his apartment, which was early
May, and that he killed Smith there.)

At their June 11 meeting, Chester noted that
Dahmer still seemed very depressed. Dahmer told
his caseworker that he preferred male sexual partners, but he felt guilty about his drives. "Subject
stated that at this time he is not involved in any
sexual activities," Chester wrote. She told him "of
the problems that can arise if he is not careful about
his sexual preferences." She made a notation that
"at this point in time plans to remain celibate." She
ended with a note that she told Dahmer to contact
gay rights organizations to talk about his feelings.
(The family of Edward Smith said he disappeared
on June 14. That date also conflicts with one Dahmer gave police. He said the two of them met
sometime in July, and that he killed Smith at his
apartment.)

The following meeting, on June 25, Chester
questioned the depth of Dahmer's problems. "Subject seems depressed all the time. May be an act.
Will monitor closely." There was also a discussion
about the neighborhood Dahmer lived in. "Told
subject he was to work on finding another apartment. Subject stated that he . . . has not had the
chance. Told subject he should look anyway." She
asked him about his sexual behavior and noted he
"denied any involvement." The next few lines are
blocked out, but Chester noted she reminded him

"of the consequences that will happen if there is any acting out." Chester was concerned enough to at least think about visiting Dahmer's one-bedroom apartment. "Will consider a home visit, but subject lives in a very bad area. If agent does home visit, will request another agent to go too," Chester wrote.

The home visit was not made.

On July 9, when Dahmer appeared in Chester's office, he was an hour late. His appearance had again deteriorated, he was depressed, and he talked about suicide. Dahmer told the caseworker he was late because he had fallen down some stairs, injured himself, and slept in. She advised him to move from the neighborhood. He also mentioned his severe financial problems and a number of hospital bills. The only known record is a bill of $324 from the West Allis Memorial Hospital in November of 1988. He said the injuries were from a mugging, but West Allis police had no record of such an incident. While talking about his lack of money, Dahmer tried to sell Chester a camera he had brought along and said he had to borrow $300 to pay his rent. "Agent believes subject is blowing his money, but not sure on what. He appears defensive if questioned where his money goes. Asked subject if he has been with someone or picking up guys. Subject states no. Falling down stairs may have been another assault on him."

Chester's notes on July 24 and July 26 deal mainly with some probation and counseling appointments Dahmer missed. She said she called him and was assured he had "no major difficulties" and has "got food in the house."

On August 13, Chester's notes indicate she talked to Dahmer about depression and suicidal urges. He indicated he was too preoccupied with a warning by West Allis Hospital that they would sue to recover the money he owed them. Dahmer agreed to pay the $324, plus $51.50 in court costs. "Most of his problems seem to be monetary," Chester wrote. She recommended he contact an attorney to discuss bankruptcy laws. "Subject again discussed the only way he can see out is to 'jump from a tall building,' " Chester wrote. She added that Dahmer said he had "too many other problems to have much of a sexual drive."

On August 27, Dahmer again appeared to be depressed. Chester concluded that the reason for his emotional state was that he refused to look at anything good in his life. "Subject continues to complain how miserable his life is. Agent tried to point out the positive things in his life, but subject is unable to accept them," she wrote. Chester said she believed part of the problem stemmed from Dahmer's unhappiness about being on probation. "Although he complies with most things, he always complains about how many other things he has to do," she wrote.

The next visit was September 10, and Chester noted that Dahmer didn't seem to be as depressed as before. She noted that she had discussed "his need to work out these sexual issues about himself through therapy." She also wrote: "He's not interested in children or young males. He said drinking was a major part of his offense." (According to the criminal complaint filed against Dahmer, he met a man named Ernest Miller on September 3 and took him back to his apartment, where, he said, he killed him by cutting his throat. He told police he put the man's biceps in the freezer and kept his skull and skeleton in his apartment.)

Dahmer visited his probation officer again on September 24. He told her he had a very bad cold "and had been sick for three to four days." He also wanted to know how he was doing on probation. Chester wrote: "Subject was told okay, but he has many serious problems both emotionally and physically that need to be addressed, and he is not trying to resolve them." (September 24 was the day David Thomas's girlfriend reported him missing to police. Dahmer told police he brought Thomas back to his apartment, but did not have sex because "the man wasn't his type." He told police he drugged and killed Thomas and disposed of the body without keeping any parts of it.)

On September 26, Dahmer called Chester to say he had been robbed at gunpoint by two men near his apartment. He said they took ten dollars and his bus pass. "This is the third time subject has been robbed," Chester noted. She advised him again to move out of the neighborhood. He said the incident made him miss a counseling appointment.

The probation officer discussed the neighborhood again at their October 8 meeting, but Dahmer said he couldn't move because his lease ran until May 1991.

On October 23, Chester noted Dahmer's attitude had not improved. "Subject's attitude is still very negative. Subject refused to look at the positive side. Subject is a chronic complainer. Explained to him he needs to prioritize his 'wants,' spending money only on what is needed versus what he wants. Subject also gets angry at people who make a lot of money, saying why are they so lucky and he 'hates' them for having so much. Subject is very materialistic and told him there are many people who make less than he and are happy with their lives."

One of the few times Dahmer seemed upbeat was in early November, after he received a phone call from his grandmother. "Subject stated his grandmother called his job looking to see how he was. Subject stated that made him feel as if someone cared," Chester wrote on November 5. She also noted that Dahmer's father was supposed to visit him that day. Dahmer told Chester he had become "used to being alone" and shunned outside activities. The probation officer told Dahmer she didn't think this was a good idea. But according to her notes, "Subject said he didn't want to go places and meet people yet."

Thanksgiving was approaching, and Dahmer's father, brother, and stepmother were supposed to come to visit. Dahmer seemed apprehensive about seeing them. "He is ashamed of his behavior and doesn't want to face his family," Chester wrote on November 19.

On December 5, Chester noted that he spent the holiday at his grandmother's and was reunited with his family. "Thanksgiving went okay. Father and new wife came from Ohio and spent the day. No major problems or confrontations." Chester said Dahmer talked about sending his mother a Christmas card because he hadn't had any contact with her for five years.

On December 17, Dahmer discussed why he felt uneasy around his family. "Subject stated is uncomfortable around his family because (1) his father is controlling (2) he has nothing in common with his brother, who attends college and (3) is 'embarrassed' about his offense," Chester wrote. "Subject did state his family is supportive of him but he still feels uncomfortable around them." Dahmer also

mentioned buying a $400 security system and again
spoke of finding a safer neighborhood.

On his visit of January 3, 1991, Dahmer said
there were no problems over the holiday.

On January 22, Chester wrote that Dahmer
"states a new offense won't occur because of the
deterrent of jail. Subject states he doesn't want to
go to jail." Chester also noted Dahmer admitted to
being gay. "Told agent that's the way he is, so 'fuck
it.' Subject still appears to be struggling with this."

Dahmer appeared to take a downward turn over
the next two weeks. On February 2, Chester wrote,
"appearance is again disheveled, unshaven, dark
circles under his eyes. He says this has to do with
having the flu and working twelve hours a day."
She pressed him to find out if he had been drinking,
but he claimed to be "too sick to drink." She also
referred him to a counselor to work out his sexual
problems and listed an ominous warning: "There is
a real danger he will reoffend." (Sometime between
then and his next visit in March, Dahmer told police, he killed Curtis Straughter. It had been six
months since he last killed; there would be seven
more victims over the next four months.)

On March 25, Chester noted that Dahmer was
"still sick, tired and exhausted last couple weeks.
Subject stated he has not done anything but go to
work and come home, staying in the house till the
next workday." There was also an upbeat note.

"He is happy his mother called him after no contact for five years. She knows he is gay and has no problems accepting it. He said they will maintain contact," Chester wrote.

On April 15, Dahmer reported no difficulties to his probation officer. (He told police he met Errol Lindsey on April 7 on a street corner near his home, then killed him in his apartment. Lindsey had gone out to get a key made.)

On April 29, Chester noted that Dahmer "continues to be morbid about his problems." She thought he was overspending again. "Again told subject he is not to buy anything for a while," and suggested to go to an agency to help him manage his finances. "Subject stated will do so, but always complains but doesn't do things to change problems. Subject doesn't want to work to change life, other than financial," she wrote.

At his May 13 visit, Dahmer told his probation officer he had been questioned by police about a murder in his apartment building. Dean Vaughn had been found strangled on May 4, but there has been no link between Dahmer and the crime.

Dahmer met again with the agent on May 27. "Subject continued to complain about everything. His grandmother is ill. Gone there to help out," Chester wrote. (He told police he was doing other chores. It was in the early-morning hours of May 27 that Dahmer said he killed fourteen-year-old Konerak Sinthasomphone, shortly after police were called to his neighborhood by residents who saw the boy wandering naked in the street. And three days earlier, on May 24, Dahmer told police, he met deaf-mute Anthony Hughes at Club 219, brought him back to the apartment, and killed him.)

The June 24 notations were brief. Chester noted that Dahmer was "working twelve hours a day again. Denied having problems." He also said he wasn't sexually involved with anyone.

On July 8, Chester wrote that Dahmer was "getting closer to being fired due to lateness and missing work. Severe financial problems. If he loses job, he says that would be a good reason to commit suicide." The probation officer pointed that out Dahmer "needs to think about getting to work on time and better his attendance." She also said she "informed him of the serious consequences if he loses his job." (Again, Dahmer had been busy the past two weeks. He told police he met Matt Turner following Chicago's Gay Pride parade on June 30, and they rode a bus back to Milwaukee. He said he killed Turner in his apartment. Dahmer also said he met Jeremiah Weinberger at a gay bar in Chicago on July 5 and rode the bus back to Milwaukee. Dahmer said he killed Weinberger in his apartment.)

Things were collapsing quickly when Dahmer called on July 16. He told Chester he had been fired on July 15 and had been drinking ever since. She told him to report to her office immediately. Dahmer told her "he has not bathed or shaved for the last three days." Chester said it didn't matter, but Dahmer never showed. He called the next day to say he had fallen asleep. (Dahmer told police on July 15 he met Oliver Lacy and killed him back in his apartment. Lacy's head and heart were found later in the refrigerator.)

Dahmer's last meeting with her was on July 18. He showed up dirty, unshaven, and talking of suicide. Chester tried to be supportive, assuring him that "things aren't as bad as they appear." She advised him to call on July 29 if he was unable to find another place to live. (Dahmer told police he met Joseph Bradehoft at a bus stop on July 19, then killed him in his apartment.)

Three days later, the police who encountered a handcuffed Tracy Edwards knocked on Dahmer's apartment door.

The city of 80,000 sits on a bluff overlooking a

8

City in Shock

Jeffrey Dahmer admitted to having seventeen victims. He actually had one more. It was the city of Milwaukee.

Milwaukee calls itself a Great City on a Great Lake. An industrial center on the western shores of Lake Michigan, it is noted for its production of beer, sausages, auto parts, and electrical equipment. The work ethic is reflected in its sports teams. The American League baseball team is the Brewers, named for the beer industry; the National Football League team from nearby Green Bay is the Packers, a tribute to the meat-packing industry.

The city of 630,000 sits on a bluff overlooking a

crescent-shaped bay that accommodates the steamers plying the Great Lakes and the St. Lawrence Seaway. It is known for a rich German heritage, and 15 percent of its population has German roots. Other ethnic groups include English, Irish, Italians, and Poles. Blacks make up about 25 percent of the city.

The city has a wholesome image, partly cultivated by the TV sitcoms *Happy Days,* about Richie Cunningham and the Fonz, and *Laverne and Shirley,* the bouncy brewery workers who produced laughs and the fictional Schotz beer.

Its gleaming skyline is dominated by the forty-two-story First Wisconsin Center, which towers over the city's checkerboard pattern of streets. About one-third of the population of Wisconsin resides here, and Mayor John Norquist's favorite one-liner is, "Without Milwaukee, Wisconsin would be Iowa."

The city has lakeshore Bradford Beach and is known for a summer party called Summerfest. There's even a "Summerfest Polka" that goes like this:

"Come to Milwaukee, how humming a city you'll see.

"Come to Milwaukee, tra-la-la-la-la-lee.

"Prosit Milwaukee, toast gaily and so free.

"Milwaukee, Milwaukee, Milwaukee, a happy place to be."

Like all cities, it has problems.

Racial tensions are part of the city's history. There were race riots in 1967, plus marches, rallies, demonstrations, and sit-ins. And there is also a grim drumbeat of real-life concerns in the black community.

The city's homicide rate has leapt 126 percent in the past five years. There were a record 165 homicides last year, a jump of 43 percent. Disturbingly, three-fourths of those murdered were black.

It is one of the most segregated cities in America.

Milwaukee has the nation's largest disparity in the ratio of unemployed whites to unemployed blacks. The state jobless rate averages about 3.8 percent; it's five times that among urban blacks.

The city also has some other dubious distinctions: lowest median income for black families, highest percentage of single-parent families, highest rate of births to black teenagers, second highest percentage of black men incarcerated.

The Jeffrey Dahmer story could have happened anywhere. But part of the horror is that it happened in Milwaukee, in America's heartland. Nobody expected it to happen here.

Like many cities, Milwaukee saw its industrial base shrink in the 1980s—about 30 percent of its manufacturing jobs were lost. Allis-Chalmers, a heavy-equipment and tractor maker, went from a peak of 6,000 jobs in the early eighties to Chapter 11 Bankruptcy in 1987, and subsequently reorganized and emerged in a much leaner form. Allen-Bradley, an electrical-equipment supplier, dropped from 6,000 jobs to 1,900.

Even Schlitz, "the beer that made Milwaukee famous," was part of the hemorrhage. Beer baron Joseph C. Schlitz opened his flagship brewery in Milwaukee in 1849, but Schlitz is no longer brewed in Milwaukee. The forty-acre property closed in 1981 after a strike, and Schlitz Malt Liquor and Old Milwaukee are now labels produced by Stroh Brewery Co. of Detroit.

Michael McGee witnessed the boarded-up homes, shuttered factories, and stores protected with iron grates multiplying in his neighborhood. So he decided to do something radical about it.

McGee is an alderman, one of the few blacks on the sixteen-member city council. An original member of the Black Panthers, McGee has founded a Black Panther Militia that he says will launch terrorist attacks in 1995 if conditions don't improve. He says his 200-strong force might roll burning tires down freeways, lob bombs during Milwaukee Bucks basketball games, and take hostages.

McGee wants the city to spend $100 million to create new jobs, increase representation for blacks by redrawing council districts, and improve the plight of blacks in general.

McGee dresses in military-style clothes and wears a hip holster that carries a slingshot. He was censured by council in 1990 for throwing a scare into the sausage industry. McGee claimed he had heard of a terrorist threat to inject rat poison in the bratwurst of Usinger's, a 111-year-old sausage empire founded by German immigrants.

The company recalled eighty thousand pounds of meat, but no poison was found. Mayor John Norquist tried to calm fears by eating a Usinger's sausage at a news conference. He called McGee a "demented fool."

Dahmer gave Michael McGee lots more chances to shout and be heard. Everything he had been saying about Milwaukee's attitudes, he said, was borne out by unpardonable police responses to a white man who killed blacks.

"In Milwaukee, it's like this: If you're white, you're right. If you're black, stay back. It's mind over matter. White people don't mind because black people don't matter. This was a hate crime. A blind man can see this was a race crime," McGee said.

He wasn't the only one saying it.

Ministers, community leaders, grief-stricken families, and everyday citizens joined voices in a single cry against bigotry in Milwaukee.

To listen to the local humor is to understand the segregated nature of the north and south sides.

Question: Why is the 16th Street Viaduct the longest bridge in the world?

Answer: Because it connects Africa with Poland.

"This is a very racist city," said Queen Hyler, the black woman who founded the group Stop The Violence. "You have a white guy killing people weekly, with bodies stacking up in a building occupied mostly by blacks, but the cops are too busy riding shotgun on the black community to pay any attention."

The Rev. Leo Champion, a Baptist minister who has held services outside Dahmer's apartment building, said the serial killings have called attention to old wounds.

"Milwaukee is a sick town and it's been swept under the carpet for years. But this has lifted up the carpet and the whole world can see the dirt," he said.

"We pay the police to protect us," said the Rev. LeHavre Buck. "We've been saying to the police something's wrong. Everybody was ignored."

People from Dahmer's neighborhood said police routinely neglected their needs.

"The police don't care around here," said Yrana Thomas.

"When you call police around here, they don't act like they're supposed to. It takes them a long time to get here," said Andrea Blackmon.

"There is a perception that the police are either not able or not willing to respond to complaints of residents in the area on many issues," said Art Heitzer, forty-three, president of the Midtown Neighborhood Association.

It was as if the city had reached a flashpoint.

"I hope this is the firecracker that sets off the whole warehouse," said neighborhood resident Pat Laur.

Several of the victims' families have sued the police department. Their loved ones were killed after police encountered Dahmer with Konerak Sinthasomphone.

Oliver Lacy's family is seeking $3 million, claiming that he would be alive if it weren't for police bigotry. "If this boy had been white, there is a high probability there would have been a more thorough investigation and Mr. Dahmer would have been taken off the streets, not left out there to sacrifice people," said David E. Wittenberg, attorney for Catherine Lacy, the victim's mother. "Our client died after police delivered that boy to Dahmer on a platter."

The family of Matt Turner from Flint, Michigan, has filed a $4.5 million claim against the police department. "If this could be a form of vindication for Matt, we're all for it," said Wadell Fletcher, Turner's stepfather. "Matt was our only son. We're left empty, with nothing."

The city did not immediately respond to the suits.

At the center of this storm is Mayor John Norquist, a Democrat elected in 1988 after Harry Maier's twenty-eight-year reign in office. Norquist's task is to put back together a city that has come apart at the seams.

He called the multiple murders "the most heinous crime committed in the history of Milwaukee."

A former assemblyman and state senator, the forty-one-year-old Norquist is the son of a preacher, and he had the strong support of blacks and Hispanics in the 1988 election. Born in Princeton, New Jersey, he earned a degree in political science in 1971 from the University of Wisconsin.

To begin to heal his city, he created a blue-ribbon citizens commission to study police-community relations, including police sensitivity, training, and improved performance in poor, high-crime neighborhoods.

"A vicious, cold-blooded, calculating killer has preyed upon our citizens. He has caused incomprehensible grief to the families of his victims. He also preyed on the minds and hearts of the entire community. The greatest tragedy of all would be for this city to be torn apart," the mayor said.

"I understand the rage that exists, especially in the area most devastated by this killer. The desire to lash out and fix blame is strong. But we must remember, one man killed his victims," Norquist said.

He called the weeks following the Dahmer discovery "perhaps the most traumatic time in Milwaukee's history." And he acknowledged that some long-festering tensions had surfaced.

"If you look at the facts that have been reported through the media, and you look at the issues around this case, there's no way you can't conclude that racial insensitivity is an issue," Norquist said. "There are cries for help that have for too long gone unheard. Let us begin to heal our wounds."

The wounds cut deeply into the city's sense of itself.

"Some of the scars of this will remain with the city for a long time," said Alderman John Kalwitz.

To help the community cope with grief, eight members of the National Organization for Victims Assistance (NOVA) were invited in. NOVA is an all-volunteer, not-for-profit group made up of psychiatrists and psychologists trained to help people deal with trauma. They stayed in Milwaukee for three days holding counseling sessions with community and church groups, and dispensing advice on how to help people cope with trauma.

The idea was to help people rebuild their lives.

"Murder is difficult in a city, but when multiple murders occur, it is clear a community can go into shock for a long time," said Marlene Young, NO-VA's executive director.

Dr. Stephanie Hurd, a psychiatrist, warned that the hurt from the Dahmer case would not go away soon, because new revelations and repeated news account bring the issues to life again and again.

"This is not a finite trauma. The community is being traumatized and retraumatized. Healing will take a long time," she said.

9

Storm over the Police Department

Police Chief Philip Arreola has been a cop for thirty-one years, but he's still thought of as an outsider by some in Milwaukee.

A native of Mexico who was raised in Detroit, he is the first Hispanic to head the city police department and the first one ever to come from outside its ranks. When he was named chief in September of 1989, he was hailed by the Fire and Police Commission as a man who would modernize the force and reach out to the community.

Arreola, fifty-one, brought with him a combina-

tion of academic credentials and street smarts ac-
quired in the tough neighborhoods of Detroit. He
has a law degree from Wayne State University in
Michigan and was a fellow in criminal justice at the
Harvard Law School.

A cop in Detroit for twenty-seven years, he
achieved the rank of commander of the 250 officers
in the Sixth District. He was no stranger to a cop's
life-or-death decisions. In 1979, when a man with a
rifle barricaded himself inside his home, Arreola
and another officer shot and killed the man when he
wheeled and pointed the rifle at them. There was
nothing else that could have been done.

Arreola, married with three daughters, left Detroit to become chief of the fifty-one-member police
force in Port Huron, Michigan, a bedroom community sixty miles away.

The Milwaukee job was the culmination of his
life's work. Some locals who also coveted the job
resented this outsider, but he was determined to run
a first-rate department, with or without friction from
his peers.

A series of killings had turned an apartment into
a murder factory, and Arreola, a trim 6-foot-2, was
eager to get to the bottom of it. It was the most
unfathomable crime he had ever come across: a
man who lured other men, drugged them, strangled
them, cut them up, devoured some human flesh,
preserved other body parts as keepsakes, flushed

remains down the toilet, and carried out human bones in garbage bags.

Jesus. They don't even write fiction this improbable. Now the horror was coming to life on the police blotters written by his own men.

Arreola's initial reaction was "obviously one of utter horror to imagine that any human being, any civilized human being in civilized society, could do something as gruesome."

The chief was on the scene at the Oxford Apartments early on the morning of July 23.

Among his first pronouncements, he praised officers Robert Rauth and Rolf Mueller for thorough police work. They had been flagged down by a man in handcuffs, then led to a foul-smelling apartment. Through curiosity and good police work, the two officers had done what others were unable to do in thirteen years—flush out Jeffrey Dahmer.

He also took some swipes at the criminal justice system—the bane of men and women who pound the pavement to protect society against criminals, only to see them slapped on the wrist and back on the streets again.

Jeffrey Dahmer was a convicted felon, yet served ten months of a work-release sentence so he could keep his nighttime job at a chocolate factory. If this man was supposed to be getting treatment for his psychological problems and his alcoholism, something wasn't working. The judge who had stayed his five-year prison sentence had even allowed him an early release from his one-year stint at the House of Correction.

This man who was admitting to seventeen murders was on probation for molesting a child. The probation officer didn't visit him every thirty days as the law required. She was overloaded with cases and Dahmer's neighborhood was pretty tough, so her supervisors approved a waiver in which Dahmer reported to her office every two weeks. Could an alert probation officer visiting the apartment have noticed the strange Polaroids and the stench of death?

Arreola called the Dahmer file "a damning indictment of the criminal justice system. Here we see the tragic results."

That claim was disputed by Roger Miller, assistant chief of the probation and parole office, who said parole officer Donna Chester had performed her duties.

"The agent did a good job, but Dahmer was a con and he conned the agent and the system," Miller said. "There were no tip-offs. He had a lot of people fooled."

The Dahmer case had put Milwaukee on the front pages, hogging national headlines from high-profile murder capitals such as New York City, Washington, Detroit, and Los Angeles. The day the story broke, Daryl Gates announced he was stepping down as police chief in Los Angeles after four of his men were videotaped kicking and clubbing a black motorist, Rodney Allen King.

Now people were accusing the Milwaukee police department of racial insensitivity. And people were making sick jokes about Arreola's new town, suggesting, for example, that they change the name of Milwaukee to Hackensack.

But the Dahmer investigation, from the top cop's standpoint, was proceeding by the book in the early days.

"I felt comfortable the investigation was going on as well as we could have expected," Arreola said.

Police were busily checking out Dahmer's story. They identified victims by matching dental records with skulls, getting fingerprints where they could, and confirming identities by showing pictures found in the apartment to relatives.

Then, Arreola's own department took its place in the headlines.

It was Thursday, July 25, when Arreola got the word. Some cops had gone to a supervisor with a disturbing tale: they had been out to Dahmer's apartment in May to check out a homosexual domestic squabble. They had contact with this guy, but they didn't suspect anything was wrong, so they let him go with his male companion. The companion was the fourteen-year-old Laotian boy who was among Dahmer's victims.

At the same time, three black women were coming forward with stories that they had called the police that same night in May, and that cops had allowed a boy to go home with Dahmer. There were concerns race played a role. Dahmer was white, the women were black, the victim was Laotian.

On Friday, Arreola sat in front of a forest of microphones. He announced he had suspended three officers with pay pending an investigation of what went on May 27. Three men, all with merit arrests in their files, were stripped of their badges and service revolvers and ID cards. Later, Arreola brought internal charges against them because he said they "failed to conduct a basic, proper police investigation into the matter." Two were dismissed.

"Personally, I was devastated," Arreola said when he learned what had happened. "I can only say it's inexplicable. It's my job to see this department is accountable to the community."

At a news conference, he was asked how it felt to have the police let Dahmer slip through their fingers before he killed Sinthasomphone and four other men.

"I wish I could put that feeling into words for you today," the chief said grimly.

"Could you try?" a reporter pressed.

"No, I cannot."

Arreola was clearly the man in the middle of a turbulent situation.

On the one hand, some members of the community were telling the chief his officers were callous toward people of color and the gay community. On the other hand, the union representing the 1,900-member city police force said the police were not given a chance to tell their side of the story. Bradley DeBraska, president of the Milwaukee Police Association, asked union members to take a vote showing their confidence in Arreola and said the chief should resign if the results were negative.

"In his rush to find a scapegoat for the recent tragedies, the chief suspended three Milwaukee police officers, knowing full well that the community would interpret the suspensions as his conclusion that they had failed to perform their duties," DeBraska said. "Even Jeffrey Dahmer gets a trial before he is convicted. Yet the chief has suspended three officers before he has even had an opportunity to ask each of them what happened. Of all people, the chief should know better."

In the vote called by DeBraska, 93.6 percent of the members of the police union voiced "no confidence" in Arreola and 98 percent of the 1,339 union members said he had wrongly suspended the three cops.

"Based on these figures, I request the chief of police to resign and let someone more competent run the department," said Robert Kliesmet, president of the International Union of Police Association.

Arreola said he had no intention of resigning. "Under no circumstances am I going to step down," the beleaguered chief said. "This is a challenge to rebuild confidence, to bridge the gap, if there is any, between ourselves and the community."

Mayor John O. Norquist knew the time had come for action. He supported Arreola's decision to suspend the officers and do an internal investigation of the entire matter. "Due to the serious nature of the allegations, an investigation is clearly warranted. I want the investigation to be thorough and to be completed as soon as possible so the questions that have been raised can be answered," the mayor said in a statement.

Later, the mayor turned up the heat.

"There can be no excuse for the way this case was reportedly handled. If these three officers are found to have acted improperly and to have betrayed the public trust, the people of Milwaukee will justifiably expect strong disciplinary action," he said.

There was talk in the police department of a job action—something like blue flu, in which a lot of cops would call in sick to protest the way their brother officers were being treated. Those threats didn't sit too well with John Tries, the mayor's chief of staff. Tries is a former cop and a former member of the Milwaukee Police Supervisors Organization.

"What are the citizens to think of a police union where members are threatening to walk out on the community at a time like this?" Tries asked.

"We would prefer to see everyone allowing the internal affairs division to proceed until a conclusion is reached. You have to assume the chief's decisions are based upon his best judgment of what is appropriate from these circumstances," Tries said.

But it was clear the case was tearing apart a fractured department. When Arreola announced internal charges had been filed against the three officers, his comments at a news conference were broadcast over police radio channels.

Dennis Forjan, president of the Milwaukee Police Supervisors Organization, defended the cops and criticized Arreola. "This is like proclaiming them guilty until proven innocent," Forjan said.

Kenneth J. Murray, an attorney for the Milwaukee Police Association, said the three officers would fight Arreola's charges. Under police department procedures, they were interviewed by the internal affairs division and given the opportunity to file written responses. The responses were not made public.

"He is feeling a lynch-mob mentality," Murray

said. "We will fight. These officers did what they were supposed to do. But based on what people see on television and read in the paper, it appears these officers screwed up."

Laurie Eggert, also a police union lawyer, said the officers had been taken in by Dahmer's coldly convincing manner.

"That man appeared to be calm, concerned for his friend, relaxed, and showed no sign of trying to hide anything, no sign of nervousness that would typically be there if a person were trying to hide a crime," she said.

"Based on everything they knew at the time, there was a caring relationship, and now we all know it was disgustingly not true. But you cannot point the finger at these officers for what we now know about Mr. Dahmer. Nobody knew. Not ten years ago. Not twenty years ago. It's not fair for anyone to second-guess what these officers did."

Eggert said the officers went up to the apartment to corroborate Dahmer's story that the companion was his friend. They were shown pictures of a smiling man modeling for pictures and shown an identification card that said he was nineteen.

"The pictures were of an Asian male in some sort of brief underwear or some type of bikini-style swimsuit. He was relaxed. He was smiling. It wasn't a torture situation. They had a picture of a relaxed, comfortable male posing in his underwear for what they believed to be his friend," Eggert said.

The three policemen were devastated when they learned the truth.

"They have been portrayed here as almost sub-human and perhaps as bad as Dahmer. People have said they didn't care about this poor fourteen-year-old kid, I can tell you that they do care. They cared back then, and they care now. They wouldn't be police officers if they didn't care," Eggert said.

Joseph Gabrish, a seven-year cop who wanted to be a policeman since he was sixteen, pledged to fight on too. He just wanted to be a good cop, and now he was caught up in a firestorm of protest.

He was one of the three officers who took part in the May 27 call outside Jeffrey Dahmer's apartment. He hoped that one day the record would be set straight.

"God is my witness, I just didn't dump a little boy in the hands of a murderer. That's not what happened," he told the *Milwaukee Journal* in an interview published August 25.

"With the set of circumstances we had on that night, we acted properly and within our training. We handled the situation as we thought it should be handled.

"I can't believe the community would believe that I would leave a young boy bleeding and just turn him over to someone, just leave without having administered any care. That just wasn't the case. We thought there was a caring relationship between these two individuals. Being homosexual is not against the law . . . and I don't base any decision on that.

"We're trained to be observant and spot things. There was just nothing that stood out, or we would have seen it. I've been doing this for a while, and usually if something stands out, you'll spot it. There just wasn't anything there. I run this thing through my mind, I just wish there would have been. There just wasn't."

He was stunned that people have accused the police department of racism and bigotry toward gays and people of color.

"It's obviously not been easy to deal with it from the beginning of the ordeal. To find out that this young man was killed shortly after we were there, that was very difficult. It became harder to deal with when I found out there were people who actually think that we would have allowed something like that to happen."

Giving up his revolver and police shield was tough. When he heard the facts in the Dahmer case, he said he went to a commander and volunteered the admission that he and others had been to the Dahmer apartment in May.

"It seemed like a part of me died. I felt I was being railroaded."

Wisconsin Attorney General James Doyle announced on August 29 that none of the officers would face criminal charges even though they may have used poor discretion.

"While in hindsight we wish the officers had handled the encounter with Dahmer differently, we are firm in our belief that they cannot be criminally prosecuted for their actions," Doyle said. "Failing to make the correct judgment is not a violation of the criminal law."

But clearly, people had lost faith in the department.

An August 4 poll commissioned by the *Milwaukee Journal* showed that 80 percent of respondents to a survey felt the police acted improperly in the May 27 incident. Among blacks, the sentiment was 93 percent.

"What do you do when the people that are supposed to be protecting us are now letting us die?" said the Rev. LeHavre Buck, an activist in the black community. "If that had been a black man chasing a white boy down the alley and dragging him back, that would never have happened. If that boy had been white, he'd be alive today. People felt completely sold out by the police after that. My mother used to say that if you were in trouble you could always call the police. I'm not sure that's true anymore."

Leaders of the gay community noted that many of the victims were gays and blacks. They said the police department had a pattern of ignoring their concerns.

"Not only were these men the victims of a mass murderer, but also of a police department that did not even notice, much less act on, the disappearance of so many young men," said Scott Gunkel of the Lambda Rights Network, a gay advocacy organization.

Black politicians and community leaders demanded an independent investigation of the police department. Things were falling apart so fast that some people urged calm.

"There's a lot of polarization in the community. Black against white, heterosexual against homosexual, the police department against the police chief, the community against the police," State Representative Gwendolynne Moore said at a news conference.

"Being angry and feeling rage is normal in the grieving process, but in order to move past that point, we've got to pull together. We cannot allow this one man to cause the implosion of our community."

She also said she was investigating reports from policemen saying that fellow officers were insensitive to minorities, calling them names like "niggers and fags."

Black policemen also had some strong opinions. Sergeant Leonard Wells, an eighteen-year veteran of the force, is president of the League of Martin, an organization of black officers named for the Rev. Dr. Martin Luther King, Jr.

"If you're poor, black, Hispanic, gay or lesbian, then in the eyes of many on the Milwaukee Police Department, you are engaging in deviant behavior," Wells said.

About 13 percent of the police force is black; blacks make up about 25 percent of the city's population as a whole.

The worst part for Arreola was that he felt he had started to make some headway in shaping his department. To a large extent, the Milwaukee Police Department is a reflection of Harold Breier, the tough law-and-order chief who held sway over the force for twenty years. He had been a cop for forty-four years when he retired in 1984.

Blacks and gays say police attitudes about their communities stem from Breier's reign. Just six months before he resigned, Breier said school busing would export crime from black neighborhoods. "We have bused crime all over the city. The south side now has black crime," he said.

A strict disciplinarian, Breier ran the force from 1964 through the Milwaukee race riots of 1967 to the days of enforced busing. His critics called him the "Milwaukee Führer." His supporters credited him with keeping the city's crime rate low while inner-city troubles raged in places like Washington, D.C., and Detroit.

"Are you a racist because you tell the truth? I figured I do what I thought was right and the hell with everything else," Breier said.

In spite of a court-approved plan to hire minorities, Breier's department had only 188 black officers in a 2,100-member department. No blacks were in command positions.

There was outrage from the black community in 1981, when a twenty-two-year-old black man died while in police custody. Police were holding him as a rape suspect, but he was later found not to have committed a crime. A subsequent investigation found that the man, Ernest Lacy (no relation to victim Oliver Lacy), died after an officer knelt on his back while he was facedown on the pavement. His hands were manacled behind him.

Lacy's death, which took place five blocks from the Oxford Apartments, sparked an uproar that led to marches and rallies. The police denied any wrongdoing. Lacy's family later received $600,000 in an out-of-court settlement with the city.

Breier staunchly defended the officers, saying an internal investigation showed the men had done nothing wrong. The force's oversight group, the Fire and Police Commission, disagreed. They fired one officer and suspended four others.

Arreola found himself in the middle of another controversy before the Dahmer case. In February 1991, he was quoted as saying the department "in the past has enjoyed the reputation of being a racist organization."

Breier criticized those remarks. So did Robert Ziarnik, Arreola's immediate predecessor, who resigned in 1989. Arreola later distributed a memo saying his remarks had been taken out of context and that he did not consider the police department to be racist.

In May, however, three white officers formed a lobbying group to combat what they saw as reverse discrimination.

Ziarnik also criticized Arreola during the Dahmer case for suspending the cops before an investigation was complete. He said his policy was to reassign people to off-street duties until all the facts were known.

During his tenure, Arreola had instituted community-based policing, trying to make officers more responsive to the neighborhoods in which they patrolled. He reestablished foot patrols in trouble spots, hoping that police presence would ease tensions. He sought to hire more minorities and promote minorities to leadership posts.

Last summer, the Milwaukee Fire and Police Commission began making it easier to file complaints against the police by removing red tape and bureaucratic roadblocks.

The U.S. Justice Department said it would address community concerns arising from the serial killings, and the FBI offered what assistance it could.

"Although at this point there appears to be no federal criminal jurisdiction, the Federal Bureau of Investigation already is providing maximum assistance to the Milwaukee police in the form of laboratory services, behavioral science experts, and coverage of out-of-state leads," Attorney General Dick Thornburgh said in a statement from Washington, D.C.

Milwaukee police officers swear two oaths when they get their badges. The first is to faithfully enforce the U.S. Constitution and the laws of Wisconsin and Milwaukee.

The second is an oath to a code of ethics. It reads in part:

As a law enforcement officer, my fundamental duty is to serve mankind; to safeguard lives and property; to protect the innocent against deception, the weak against violence or disorder, and to respect the constitutional rights of all persons to liberty, equality and justice.

I will never act officiously or permit personal feelings,

prejudices, animosities or friendships to influence my decisions. With no compromise for crime and with relentless prosecution and appropriately without fear or favor, malice or ill will, never employing unnecessary force or violence and never accepting gratuities.

I recognize the badge of my office as a symbol of public faith, and I accept it as a public trust to be held so long as I am true to the ethics of police service. I will constantly strive to achieve these objectives and ideals, dedicating myself to my chosen profession . . . law enforcement.

On September 6, Chief Philip Arreola announced at a news conference that he had dismissed officers John Balcerzak and Joseph Gabrish and placed Richard Porubcan on a year's probation. Arreola said the officers failed to follow basic procedures in the incident. The police union said it would appeal. "Their memo books contained almost no information pertaining to the assignment and the investigation they purported to undertake," Arreola said. He added that the officers "failed to take an obviously incapacitated child into custody."

10

Cries from All Sides

The splintering of Milwaukee was evident in the rallies that were being held almost daily in early August.

Some rallied in support of the beleaguered police department, which some had accused of being negligent and insensitive. Hispanic groups rallied in support of Police Chief Philip Arreola after the police union demanded his resignation. Families of victims, black leaders, and gay groups marched in a candlelight vigil to address their wounds.

It was as if the city were having a collective nervous breakdown.

"I think the city is traumatized. There's a massive, melancholic introspection going on. The whole city is having a depressive bout," said Dr. Ashok Bedi, clinical director of the Milwaukee Psychiatric Hospital.

For example, police advocates launched Operation Blue Ribbon to show support for the police department and to protest the suspensions of the three officers. About two hundred people, mostly police officers and their wives, marched on City Hall on Sunday, August 5. Many wore blue ribbons to show their support for the people who are out in the streets every day, putting their lives on the line for law and order.

"If the police officers in this city are not judged fairly and with compassion, a part of this city will never recover," said Alderwoman Annette E. Scherbert.

Alderman Robert Anderson also addressed the crowd. "What is the status of the mayor's office? For us or not?" Anderson said.

The crowd hooted, hissed, and booed lustily to show their feelings for Mayor John Norquist.

"There's no way, in any way, that we can go against the police department. Until we die, we stick together," Anderson said.

The crowd waved hand-made placards that read: WE SUPPORT OUR COPS—DO YOU? and MY DAD'S A GOOD COP and OUR POLICE SAVE AND PROTECT.

Bradley DeBraska, president of the Milwaukee

Police Association, noted that 94 percent of the police union had no confidence in Arreola. "They don't want this guy. Send him back to Detroit," he said.

It went without saying that morale in the department had plummeted to an all-time low.

Few were cheering for the police at a different kind of rally the next day. Friends and families of victims had gathered to share their collective anger, anguish, and grief. There were painful feelings that needed to be addressed.

One of the placards held aloft at a candlelight vigil summed up the attitudes of many. It was made in the form of a police badge and contained the pictures of Dahmer's victims. It said, MILWAUKEE POLICE—PAID TO PROTECT ALL PEOPLE.

A crowd of four hundred people gathered for the vigil that began at Juneau Park, named for the French trapper who first settled in Milwaukee. There were speeches and prayers before the group marched, singing "We Shall Overcome," to MacArthur Park outside the county courthouse.

"We aren't here to discuss the police," said Annabelle Havlicek, one of the rally's organizers. "We aren't here to discuss politics. We're here to remember the victims—and with everyone else to rebuild the community of Milwaukee."

Emotions were raw.

Alderman Paul Henningsen, who represents the district where Dahmer lived, was among the speakers. But he found it difficult to relate to the crowd.

"There are many people angry in Milwaukee today. Are you angry?"

"Yes," the crowd shouted back.

"There are many people frustrated in Milwaukee today. Are you frustrated?"

"Yes," again came the reply, a little lower.

"Are you ready to look beyond tragedy? Are you ready to stare evil in its face? Are you ready to go above it, around it, through it? We must pull together or Milwaukee—and all of you—will be another victim. We must understand that the person whose name we know all too well . . ."

A black man wearing a tag that said FAMILY interrupted the blond speaker with a shout. "Don't say his name. Don't you say it."

Henningsen pressed on.

"We cannot be enemies of the police."

"Why not?" someone screamed. The crowd was booing Henningsen now. "Don't you defend them. Don't you dare even try to defend them. They're to blame," someone else said.

"We can't let our anger victimize us," Henningsen said.

Donna Burkett had heard enough. She is a cousin of Tony Hughes, the deaf-mute who Dahmer said he met in a gay bar and then killed in his apartment.

"They're talking bullshit," Burkett said.

"They're trying to take our anger away, so we'll forget. Well, we don't want to forget and we don't want to calm down. We want to keep our anger until justice is done. We want to see the police charged and everyone charged who was an accessory after the fact."

Will that be justice, she was asked?

"No. We won't see justice until we can see police who treat everyone the same and care about everyone, everyone on the streets. But that would be a first step."

She shouted at Henningsen, "We want justice!" Then she turned and broke down in tears.

Tony Hughes's mother, Shirley, clutched a Bible and wore a picture of her son on her blouse. She also wore a stick-on name tag that said FAMILY. She was surrounded by cousins and sisters as she sat on the stage listening to the speakers. A gaggle of photographers, five across and three deep, perched in front of her.

When the woman began to weep, a young girl put her arms around her in comfort. The photographers moved in closer for better shots, jostling and pushing each other out of the way. Mrs. Hughes sobbed more deeply, and another family member came over to give a comforting embrace. The photographers pushed in closer, shutters clicking like excited locusts. Those who didn't have a good position climbed on stage in front of a speaker. A rally organizer came down and asked them not to be so hard on the family in a moment of grief.

The shutters snapped away until the next speaker made an announcement for all media to clear out of the front rows. Another person came down and started clearing them out. Nobody moved too far, but they stopped taking as many pictures.

Cheryl Franklin, a community activist, took the stage as things calmed down. "It's time for us to make a change in the way we look at each other and the way we look at ourselves," she said when order was restored. "We must start together. Together we must put people in our circle of one. Look at their hearts. Look at their eyes. We need to get together, people, today."

Queen Hyler, founder of Stop The Violence, was next. "Why did such a terrible thing happen? How could anyone commit such hideous crimes against another human being?"

Then she spoke about long-existing problems that Jeffrey Dahmer had dredged to the surface. "We must face the cold, hard facts that racism is very much alive in this city. Minorities and gays and others are still treated as second-class citizens. This one case has opened so many wounds. It's easy to see racism in the work force, in the police department, and everywhere. It's very blatant, but no one wants to hear it. How can you heal something unless you admit that it exists?

"My patience is beginning to wear out. I've been in this role of fighting racial injustice too long, and soon every role must wear out. If any police officer—"

Someone shouted back. "They're just KKK members."

"If any police officer puts on a uniform and vows to uphold the law, that is what I expect them to do, regardless of one's race or appearance," Hyler said.

"I will remember the clean appearance of Jeffrey Dahmer in the court, his lack of emotion, his lack of remorse, until the day I die," she continued. "These victims' deaths cannot and must not be in vain."

One woman in the crowd wore a button that read: GOOD NEIGHBORS COME IN ALL COLORS.

Next to speak was Mayor John Norquist. While he was being introduced, and while he waited silently for the crowd to settle before he talked, there were murmurs in the group.

"You better say the right thing. You better speak right. We put you into office and we can put you out," someone shouted at him.

Norquist spoke briefly. He said the police actions were under investigation, and he commended

Glenda Cleveland, the typesetter who persisted when the police turned away.

The mayor praised her as a woman "who showed the community what it really means to be a good and decent citizen, and a model citizen for everyone."

Stephanie Hume, one of the vigil organizers, said the rally was designed with healing in mind. "We needed to put together this vigil for the community to be able to come and share their feelings and get over the pain and anger of what happened," Hume said.

Organizers made sure everyone had a three-inch white candle with a paper holder before the one-mile march down Kilbourn Avenue to MacArthur Square. It was about 8 P.M.; the last remaining beams of sunlight were dying out. The candlelight made a powerful image in the dark, and the mood swung from anger to quiet reflection as the rally-goers snaked their way to the square.

More speakers got up. As always, they were accompanied by signers for the deaf, a remembrance of the way Tony Hughes communicated, along with his cheery smile.

Two of the speakers were seventeen-year-old friends of Curtis Straughter, another murder victim. "I'm black and I'm proud, and I'm gay and I'm proud," said one. He didn't give his name for fear of being identified in the media and harassed.

"But my friend will never grow old. He'll never get the chance. He was a true friend to me and all the gay community. But we deserve the chance to grow old. Young black men today are scared. Gay men are scared. Curtis made a mistake. He went somewhere he shouldn't have gone with someone he shouldn't have been with. He was trusting. All I can say is be careful. Have better judgment."

One of the speakers was Jeanetta Robinson, founder and director of Career Youth Development, who was a veteran on the civil rights marches of the sixties. Here it was the nineties, and the same evils still lurked in the world.

"The duty of everyone here is to see that some good comes out of this tragedy. It is us, the people here, who must do it ourselves. Yes, we thank God we have a wonderful police chief, but unfortunately, he inherited some police officers who have violent tendencies. We are going to demand that the insensitive police officers, be they black or white, be better trained in cultural and sex differences. When I was a little girl marching with Martin Luther King, I thought it would all be over in a while, but now I know it's a never-ending thing. In Milwaukee, black kids are killing black kids every day. People are calling the police, but nobody answers. Grief is hard to take. We must all work together, blacks and whites, homosexuals and heterosexuals, to get through this tragedy. But because of this tragedy, we are together tonight. We want to blame each other, but we can't be black against white or this against that. We're going to unite, and together we will demand justice.''

Shirley Hughes gathered her strength to express her feelings. She prayed for healing in the community.

"I urge you, please don't hold hatred in your hearts, just pray and ask God for help," Mrs. Hughes said. "Tony loved everyone and everyone loved Tony."

Two days later, she walked through the streets on the arm of the Rev. Jesse Jackson, who was coming from Washington, D.C., to comfort the afflicted and afflict the comfortable.

Jesse Jackson was a preacher and a community activist long before he made two unsuccessful bids for the Democratic presidential nomination. He came to preach in Milwaukee, to minister to grieving families, to pray for the victims, to seek justice, to rail against police insensitivities, to condemn racism and crime. It was a seven-hour whirlwind stop.

"There's a lot of brokenness in the community now. Broken hearts and broken dreams and broken relationships. There is lots of distrust. Yet in all this we must have the will to pick up the pieces and turn to each other and rely on each other and thank God for what's left so that our children might not be so vulnerable.

"This matter has real overtones of racism. This is an opportunity as well as a challenge, while America is watching, to maybe address America from Milwaukee."

Jackson pressed for a thorough investigation of police responses, saying the gap between the police and the community had to be bridged. He pointed to the underlying reasons why the victims were so vulnerable—poor education, joblessness, crime, drugs, racism—and noted these elements exist in all cities.

"When your back is against the wall, you must not accept darkness like it will be dark always," Jackson said.

Jackson went to the Oxford Apartments, praying on the grassy slope outside the notorious landmark where Jeffrey Dahmer lived. He met with Glenda Cleveland, the woman who repeatedly questioned the police about allowing a naked, bleeding Laotian boy to go with Dahmer on May 27.

"All that we want is equal protection under the law. The game should be played under one set of rules," Jackson said.

He marched to a rally at St. Luke's Emmanuel Baptist Church, where he took to the pulpit. "Preach, Jesse. Say it," the congregation told him.

Jackson called the no-confidence vote by the

police union against Chief Arreola a "public mutiny." Jackson urged people to support the chief, and they responded by chanting "Don't step down."

During his stay, he raised $5,000 to help victims' families pay for burial costs.

That same week, the Hispanic Chamber of Commerce came out in support of Arreola.

"A vast majority of the Hispanic Community is behind him. We think he's doing an incredibly good job under the circumstances," said chamber director Maria Monreal-Cameron.

She also said her group would press for better relations with the police. "We are never going to wipe out prejudice and racism in the department," Monreal-Cameron said. "There is no way to eliminate it. But we are going to call the police department to task on it whenever racism comes up."

Abel R. Ortez, executive director of a Hispanic group called Jobs for Progress, said the head of the police union should resign for its criticism of Arreola. "We are dismayed by the actions of the police union. They only serve to divide an already traumatized community," Ortez said.

In an attempt to bind his fractured city, Mayor Norquist called for a city-wide day of healing on Sunday, August 11.

"It hurts you to your soul that this tragedy has come into our community. Your whole being hurts," said the Rev. LeHavre Buck. "You want to cry. You want to holler. You want to blame somebody for this pain. The city is in mourning. Every mother and father is saying, 'That could have been my child.'

"We didn't need death. We've got enough of that already."

11

Gay Bashing

There was consternation in the gay community. Some of Jeffrey Dahmer's victims were gay, and there was grieving for those who died. There was anger that it could have happened. And there was outrage because they were somehow being blamed for what happened.

One anonymous letter, postmarked July 26, was addressed to the executive editor of the *Wisconsin Light*, a newspaper serving the gay and lesbian community: "I don't care if you queers die of AIDS or dismemberment. Do us all a favor and hurry it up, okay? I hope Dahmer gets off on a technicality."

The blinking light on the answering machine, also on July 26, heralded this message for Dan Schramm, president of Gay/Lesbian International News Network. "Hello, this is Jeffrey Dahmer. I want your head in my refrigerator. Call me."

Scott Gunkel, president of the Lambda Rights Network, also had heard an unfamiliar voice on his answering machine on July 30, the day after he held a news conference condemning the backlash against gays. "You got what you deserved. You're going to get more of it. If you don't shut up, you'll be next."

The M&M Club, a gay bar on North Water Street, received two bomb threats after the story broke on the serial killings. People walking outside Club 219 on Second Street were pelted with eggs thrown from a passing convertible.

Cars drove past the gay clubs and hurled taunts.

"Goddamn faggots."

"Fucking queers."

It was all part of a backlash against gays caused, at least indirectly, by the Dahmer story. Dahmer told his family, probation officer, and a judge that he was a homosexual. Yet he told others he hated homosexuals and agonized over his own sexual orientation.

In his admissions to police, he said he lured victims from Chicago's Gay Pride Parade and gay bars in Chicago and Milwaukee. His victims were often sex partners: with four of them, it was after they were dead.

And now, besides being hunted down by a serial killer, gays were targets of more hatred.

"We've been seen as the perpetrators of this crime, when in fact, we are the victims," said Scott Gunkel. "He was stalking us. He was using us as a feeding ground."

Lesbians and gay men have made major strides toward equality and freedom by organizing and coming out of the closet. But with increased visibility, with people knowing who they are and where they're located, there has been a backlash of antigay violence.

According to a 1987 report on hate crime sponsored by the U.S. Department of Justice, "The most frequent victims of hate violence today are blacks, Hispanics, Southeast Asians, Jews, and gays. Homosexuals are probably the most frequent victims."

Dahmer targeted four of those groups.

Being picked on is a fact of life for homosexuals. Antigay violence was documented by the National Gay and Lesbian Task Force in a 1984 survey. Of 2,000 people contacted, 19 percent said they had been punched, hit, kicked, or beaten at least once in their lives because of their sexual orientation. Forty-four percent said they had been threatened with physical violence, and 94 percent said they experienced some type of victimization.

Dahmer had found a pool of invisible victims, men that either weren't missed, or if they were, did not get a lot of attention in the mainstream.

"Gay men tend to be more vulnerable," said Tim Drake of the privacy and civil rights project of the National Gay and Lesbian Task Force. "If they disappear, they are not as likely to be reported missing. If they are reported as missing, they are not as likely to get the same type of police follow-up as a report of someone's daughter, husband, or wife would get.

"We need to be more aware we are at risk. Gay men in particular are at risk for murder," said Kevin Berrill of the National Gay and Lesbian Task Force. "Killers just don't go randomly kill other people. Certain groups are targeted—certain despised and disposable groups. We can't ignore the fact that there are homicidal individuals out there who hate gays and want to kill them. We ignore those risks at our own peril."

In Milwaukee, gays made the same charges that blacks did about police neglect and bias. Police either were slow to respond or paid them no mind at all.

"It's pretty clear that if the people disappearing had been white daughters of middle-class people, the police would have been doing a thorough state-wide search until they found out who was responsible," said Dan Fons of Queer Nation/Milwaukee.

"Because it was a lot of black men, some of them known to be gay, it was ignored completely. It should have been stopped much earlier. The police make it very clear that if you live the gay lifestyle, you deserve whatever you get. As long as they think it's a bunch of gay people hurting each other, it really doesn't deserve their attention."

The Dahmer case happened right after authorities applied the term "homosexual overkill" to an earlier unrelated killing and dismemberment. In that case Joachim Dressler was charged with the murder of James Madden, twenty-four, of Whitefish Bay in Racine County.

Milwaukee County Medical Examiner Jeffrey M. Jentzen said the term applies to using much more force than is needed to kill someone. In testimony, he said "homosexual overkill" is done by a man with deeply repressed homosexual feelings or a homosexual who acted in a frenzy against a gay lover. When questioned at a news conference about the Dahmer case, he said the term didn't apply.

Gay groups challenged the use of the phrase, saying it has no more meaning than "heterosexual overkill" would in sex crimes.

"The terminology used by the authorities and by the media has emphasized and reinforced the worst stereotypes of gays and has equated our lives

with murder and violence," said Kitty Barber, president of the Lesbian Alliance of Greater Milwaukee.

"The truth is that we have loving, caring, and
gentle relationships with our partners, our families,
our friends, and our coworkers. We don't know if
the killer is gay or not. His sexual orientation is
irrelevant. His behavior is deviant by any standard.
And the fact that some of his victims were gay does
not add or subtract from the horror of his crimes,
but it does make clear that these were crimes of
hate—hatred of gay men and especially gay men of
color. Blacks and Asians and gays and poor families
are not disposable people. Where we live, who we
love, and the color of our skin does not make us
responsible for these crimes against us, nor does it
make our lives any less valuable."

Scott Gunkel, a bartender at Club 219, noted
that at a time when families were filing missing-
persons reports, the police were more concerned
about raiding strip shows at bars. Thirteen citations
for disorderly conduct were issued by thirty cops
who raided a "Hot Buns" contest March 28 at the
club.

The Dahmer case dominated conversations at
Club 219, the M&M Club, the Phoenix, C'Est La
Vie, the Wreck Room, and other gay bars. Dahmer
frequented the clubs, but he didn't come to mingle.
He usually sat at the bar, drinking alone, hardly
ever talking to anyone. He always seemed distant,

a man on the periphery. Sometimes he'd hang around the bus stop outside Club 219, where kids—some hardly older than boys—stood to attract the men cruising in their cars for tricks. Those outsiders were too young to drink legally or couldn't afford the cover charge. Gunkel remembers Dahmer standing out there on the fringe, talking to the boys at the bus stop. Only later did he find out that Dahmer was hunting humans.

People just couldn't get enough information on the story of the gay stalker. Interest ran so high that the biweekly gay newspaper printed a special edition for the first time in its four-year history.

"This guy took off after the ones in our community who were the most susceptible, the most vulnerable, the ones least able to defend themselves," said Terry Boughner, executive editor of the *Wisconsin Light*.

"We seem to be the last minority that some feel it's accepted to persecute. For us, homophobia is a fact of life. But who is going to think in their wildest imaginings something like this is going on."

One of the regulars on the gay scene who had contact with Dahmer was John Paul Ranieri, a layman with the Episcopal Church who is a self-described street minister catering to gays. The church does not support him financially, but some members donate money so he can reach out to troubled souls discarded to the streets. Those he sees are the ones with no place else to turn.

Ranieri is no stranger to the streets. A former drug addict, he worked for years as a male prostitute on the mean streets of New York City. And he was no stranger to Jeffrey Dahmer.

Several things stood out in two conversations he had with Dahmer. First, he was an angry, abusive drunk. And though he cruised the gay bars, he professed to hate gays and blacks. Dahmer believed that God sent AIDS as revenge on the gay lifestyle. "He hated the gay community with a passion, calling them 'fucking faggots.' He especially hated black queens," Ranieri said.

Dahmer tried to pick him up, Ranieri said. But he and others spread the word to stay away from Dahmer because he was a lush with a deep-seated hatred of gays. This was a man with a tortured psyche.

"I had the feeling he was emotionally hurt. He was upset all the time in bars, like he didn't want to be there but like he was compelled to be there by some inner feelings he was trying to repress. Because he couldn't deal with it, he would turn around and get drunk," Ranieri said.

"In his own mind, he used the platform of gay bars to eliminate gay men," the bearded street minister said. "It is the ultimate in gay bashing."

In the aftermath of the revelations, the National

Gay and Lesbian Task Force issued the following statement on July 29:

The grisly murders of at least seventeen men by Jeffrey L. Dahmer are another example how hatred destroys the lives of gay people and people of color. As this story has unfolded, it has become clear that many of Dahmer's victims were gay men and that most if not all were men of color. It also appears that antigay and racial bias on the part of the Milwaukee police allowed the murder toll to mount.

Although gay people were among Dahmer's victims, biased statements on the part of police and some media have linked his murderous behavior to all gay and lesbian people. For example, the term "homosexual overkill" has been used repeatedly by the police and the press in connection with the case, without any definition or explanation. Such vague and dangerous terms falsely equate killing with homosexuality. Meanwhile, similar associations are never made for "heterosexual crimes." When, for example, has the term "heterosexual overkill" ever been used to describe the serial killing of women by a male perpetrator? By confusing victims with perpetrators, media and police statements have unwittingly fostered an atmosphere of intolerance that has led to a dramatic increase in antigay harassment and threats in Milwaukee and perhaps elsewhere as well.

By failing to clearly point out that Dahmer singled out gay men for murder, the media have missed an important dimension of this story, which is that these crimes were hate-motivated. By focusing on Dahmer's alleged homosexual identity, it has overlooked the fact that many of his victims were homosexual. Regardless of Dahmer's actual sexual identity, it is clear that he hates homosexuals enough to want to kill them. It is also apparent Dahmer's murders were racially motivated.

Antigay and racial hatred are not innate characteristics. They are learned. Dahmer's behavior is the most extreme example of this type of hatred. To ignore the identity of the victims, the motivations of the murders, and the social context in which these killings take place is to ignore society's complicity in these crimes.

We are also disturbed about the apathy shown by the Milwaukee police department in connection with this case. According to Milwaukee gay and lesbian organizations, prior to Dahmer's arrest, local police failed to adequately investigate the disappearance of gay men, some of whom were his victims. This pattern of neglect was illustrated by the shocking revelation that Milwaukee police officers declined to intervene in the case of a young Laotian man who had been sexually assaulted and subsequently murdered by Dahmer. Rather than make an investigation and arrest, the officers allegedly dismissed the incident as a homosexual "lovers' quarrel." This cynical response unfortunately typifies the way in which the criminal justice system devalues the lives of gay people, people of color, and the poor.

The National Gay and Lesbian Task Force Policy Institute joins the Milwaukee gay and lesbian community in calling for (1) a full investigation of the Milwaukee police department's response to these murders and to gay and minority concerns in general, (2) the appointment of an official liaison with the Milwaukee police department to work with gay and people of color communities, and (3) the adoption of gay and minority awareness training for all Milwaukee police officers and recruits. We also call on the Milwaukee police and other local and state law enforcement agencies to initiate efforts to document and respond to hate crimes.

12

Horror Stories

A horror movie named *Body Parts* opened nationally August 2, but Paramount Pictures Corp. pulled TV ads for it in Milwaukee because of a company policy regarding sensitivity to community issues. At least one chain in Wisconsin decided not to show the movie in its theaters.

"It was out of sympathy. We're not going to do anything to distress anybody," said Paramount spokesman Harry Anderson.

Body Parts has nothing to do with serial killers who cut up their victims. It is based on the novel *Choice Cuts*, in which a criminal psychologist loses an arm in an accident. A replacement arm turns out to be the limb of a convicted murderer, and the limb still has evil motivations.

But advertisers feared the title may have conjured up coincidental connections to the Dahmer case "because of the nature of the tragedy."

But there was another ad placed in some newspapers that caused much more of a stir. It read:

"Milwaukee . . . July 1991 . . . They were drugged and dragged across the room. . . . Their legs and feet were bound together. . . . Their struggles and cries went unanswered. . . . Then they were slaughtered and their heads sawn off. . . . Their body parts were refrigerated to be eaten later. . . . It's still going on. If this leaves a bad taste in your mouth, become a vegetarian."

A tabloid version of the Milwaukee case? No, it was an ad placed in the *Des Moines Register* by an animal-rights group called People for the Ethical Treatment of Animals.

"Abuse is abuse regardless of species," said Kathy Guillermo, lifestyles campaign director for PETA. "We hope it will jolt a few people into realizing that what happened to those people is no different than what happens to animals."

She said the ad was deliberately written to be shocking.

"Most people don't have any realistic notion about the origin of the piece of meat on their tables," Guillermo said.

Dave Mehlaff, spokesman for the National Pork Producers Council, called it sickening. "It's not just tasteless, it's an obscenity. For them to try to capitalize on this shocking tragedy in Milwaukee, we think is sick and demented. It's an insult not only to the victims and their families, but to all livestock producers."

The *Milwaukee Sentinel* refused to run the ad, so PETA placed it in Iowa because there are a large number of slaughterhouses there. It cost $11,200.

Some readers called the *Register* to complain about the contents. "We are getting some calls from people who are upset, but a majority are coming away with an understanding that we have an obligation to run it," said Nancy Jo Trafton-Dyer, national advertising manager for the newspaper. "We are providing a vehicle for free speech. As long as it is not fraudulent or unlawful or libelous, we are obligated to accept it," she said.

Milwaukee Mayor John Norquist called the ad "disgusting."

Paul Obis, publisher of the *Vegetarian Times*, also was critical of it. "It exceeds the boundaries of good taste. I don't think you need to play up how terrible slaughter is, and you certainly don't need to draw parallels."

Lionel Dahmer sought to give his ailing mother some privacy too. He tacked a note on the door of her West Allis home after an avalanche of phone calls and reporters knocking on the door. He complained that some cameras were videotaping through the window blinds. A police car sat outside the home for a time to shoo away the hordes.

His July 24 note read: "Please do not ring the doorbell or phone. [A Milwaukee reporter] woke us up at 7:30 A.M. after a very hard night of stress and crank calls. Catherine Dahmer cannot endure more harassment. She is 87 years old, just recovering from pneumonia, and had her car damaged and a very recent accident. She really cannot put up with the stress of media people such as yesterday and this morning."

Reporters came from Germany, France, and England to probe revelations that Jeffrey Dahmer killed and dismembered seventeen people, saving some body parts in his apartment.

Several weeks later, Lionel Dahmer hired a private investigator to stay at his mother's. Police reported that someone driving by pelted the home with raw eggs.

The mutilation murders revived the debate over whether Wisconsin should have a death penalty. The state banned capital punishment in 1853. It didn't want any repeats of the carnival-like atmosphere that surrounded the last execution. More than one thousand people showed up to watch John

McCaffary hang in Kenosha in 1851 for drowning his wife.

Wisconsin is one of the thirteen states without a death penalty. Attempts have been made since 1937 to bring it back, but no bills have gotten past a legislative committee.

Recent polls indicate that 65 percent of Wisconsinites favor a death penalty, and Governor Tommy Thompson has said he supports capital punishment for certain heinous crimes.

State Senator Joanne Huelsman introduced legislation in 1990 to bring back the death penalty. "If you truly believe that life is important, then there has to be a significant penalty for the taking of a life. That's really what it boils down to."

But reviving the death penalty wasn't the only legislative remedy proposed. State Representative Gregory Huber planned to introduce a bill that would make it a separate crime to mutilate, disfigure, or dismember a corpse. The crime would be punishable by as much as twenty years in prison and a $10,000 fine. An additional ten years in prison and a $10,000 fine could be levied for hiding a body.

Everything about Jeffrey Dahmer drew attention—even what he wore and didn't wear to court when murder charges were filed against him.

At his first hearing, on July 25, Dahmer wore a button-down short-sleeve shirt, with wide blue stripes on a white background. His unshaven face showed three days of scraggly growth.

Some people wondered why Dahmer wasn't wearing the traditional orange coveralls that other criminal suspects wear to court. He also wasn't handcuffed or shackled.

Queen Hyler of Stop The Violence said it was just another example of subtle racism. "You have somebody who committed seventeen murders and he's not a threat. What do you have to do to be a threat? If this was a black man, they'd want his head," she said.

It became enough of an issue that the Milwaukee County Sheriff's Department distributed a statement saying that they weren't responsible for Dahmer's dress because he wasn't in their custody.

"It is the policy of the Milwaukee County Sheriff's Department that all persons who are in our care will make all court appearances in orange coveralls and restraints, if necessary," the statement said.

Dahmer wore the orange suit in his next two appearances.

Dahmer's bail was originally set at $1 million cash. On August 6, it was raised to $5 million when eight murder charges were added to the four he was charged with at the first hearing. Prosecutors filed three additional murder charges against Dahmer on August 20, putting the total at fifteen.

Each murder charge carries a mandatory life sentence. With each count of murder, Dahmer was also charged with habitual criminality because he was a convicted felon. Each of those charges tacks on ten years to each murder count.

The longest sentence he uttered at any of the preliminary hearings was, "I understand, your honor." The judge had asked him if he was aware of the charges against him.

Dahmer packed the courtroom every time he appeared. In addition to the hordes of media, the citizenry came just to get a look at this guy. Families of victims also came. About sixty of them sat shoulder to shoulder at the August 6 hearing, holding hands as the charges were detailed.

"I'm here because I want to know why," said Shirley Hughes, whose deaf-mute son, Tony, was murdered. "I wanted to see the man who killed my son to see if I could understand why it happened."

Lucy Robertson, grandmother of twenty-three-year-old David Thomas, also wanted to get a look. "I just saw that he was a human being. Just like you and me. God made him. Just as surely as God made the devil."

Dahmer is jailed alone in an eight-by-twelve foot cell. During the daytime, he can spend time in a dayroom to stretch, listen to music, or watch TV. He has a deputy watching him twenty-four hours a day. The nickname given him by other inmates as the Milwaukee County Jail? The Chop-Chop Man.

Jeffrey Dahmer has no job, no car, and no money. But he has already been sued twice for $3 billion.

Attorney Thomas M. Jacobson filed two lawsuits on behalf of the families of Ernest Miller and Curtis Straughter. The suit seeks to pay the families if Dahmer is paid any money for the rights to his story by publishers or movie producers. Wisconsin law provides that any profit from a crime be placed in an escrow account, but families must take legal steps to collect their share.

''The billion is really meant to quantify the horror and the loss to the family,'' Jacobson said. ''The money tells people how bad the harm is.''

Gerald Boyle is one of the most visible lawyers in Wisconsin. Now that he's defense counsel for Jeffrey Dahmer, he's one of the most visible in the country.

Boyle, the oldest son of an Irish Catholic family from Chicago's West Side, represented Dahmer in 1988 when he was charged with the sexual assault of a thirteen-year-old boy. Dahmer's prison sentence was stayed, and he served ten months in a work-release program.

''Every lawyer knows he can't refuse to take a

case simply because of the notoriety or the unpopularity that might go with it," Boyle said. "The scope of the crime doesn't make any difference."

As a county prosecutor in 1967, Boyle successfully put away one of Milwaukee's most notorious murderers, Michael Lee Herrington. He was convicted of the stabbing deaths of a ten-year-old girl and an eighteen-year-old woman, plus the attempted murder of a woman who escaped his attacks.

Boyle later represented former major-league baseball player Reggie Jackson when a Milwaukee man said Jackson attacked him in a bar. No charges were ever filed against Jackson.

In the Dahmer case, Boyle is paired against a former political rival in District Attorney E. Michael McCann. Both of them were county prosecutors when they resigned in 1968 to run for district attorney. McCann beat Boyle by four thousand votes in the Democratic primary, then won the post in the general election.

Boyle has conceded his client is "a very sick young man who has many kinds of mental problems." As far as preparing a defense based on a plea of insanity, Boyle said, "We are clearly investigating the mental aspect of this matter to find out what might be available to protect Mr. Dahmer's legal rights.

"My aim is to see that justice is done. I took an

oath to the principles of justice," Boyle said. "I think that regardless of all the publicity, that if everyone follows the dictates of the law, Mr. Dahmer's rights will be protected, including his rights to a fair trial."

No multiple murder in Wisconsin ever passes without a reference to Ed Gein, whose ghoulish deeds inspired the character of Norman Bates in Alfred Hitchcock's *Psycho* and Buffalo Bill in the recent movie *The Silence of the Lambs*.

Dahmer's neighbor Yrana Thomas invoked Gein's name well before the grisly discoveries, when she complained to the building manager about the pervasive stench in the Oxford.

"I asked the manager a year ago, 'Do you have another Ed Gein down there?' " Thomas said.

There are a few similarities.

Gein scratched out a living as a handyman-farmer on a 160-acre spread with his brother, Henry, near Plainfield in central Wisconsin. Their ailing mother, Augusta, had lectured them since they were boys that all other women were wicked, and she convinced her boys not to marry but to care for her and the farm instead.

Mrs. Gein died in 1945 after a second stroke, and brother Henry perished the next year while fighting a forest fire. Ed Gein was left alone.

He sealed off his mother's bedroom and the

parlor, living in his small bedroom and the kitchen. The Spartan place had no electricity or plumbing. As a recluse, he read detective magazines and anatomy textbooks, especially those sections dealing with women. He dug up female bodies from remote graves to cut them apart and study their organs. Ultimately, Gein was hoping for a sex-change operation.

A dim-witted neighbor named Gus, told that he would be helping advance the cause of science, helped Gein dig up bodies for experiments. But Gus never saw what happened after they were hauled to a shed next to the farmhouse. Gein skinned them and draped the flesh over himself, sometimes wearing the hides for hours. He dissected the bodies and kept some parts as trophies—the heads, sex organs, hearts, livers, and various strips of skin that fascinated him. He buried the bones and burned the parts he disliked.

After a time he tired of robbing graves and decided to pursue fresh bodies. Later he admitted to two murders, and both victims resembled his dead mother. He couldn't remember if he killed others or just dug them up.

The first was Mary Hogan, fifty-one, who ran a saloon in Pine Grove. One winter evening in 1954, Gein walked into the empty bar with a .22-caliber pistol and shot her in the head without saying a word. He took the body back to the farm on a sled.

In November of 1957, he killed his next victim—Mrs. Bernice Worden, operator of a hardware store for the seven hundred residents of Plainfield. Mrs. Worden's son, Frank, was the town's deputy sheriff.

One Saturday morning, with Frank and most of the menfolk off hunting deer, Gein entered the store and picked up a .22-caliber rifle from a gun rack. He brought along a single bullet and used it to kill Mrs. Worden. He drove the body back to the farm in his pickup truck.

Frank Worden discovered the store locked and his mother missing that night. The last entry in the sales book was for a half-gallon of antifreeze, a product that Gein had mentioned purchasing the night before. The sheriff went to investigate.

At the farm seven miles away, authorities made a gruesome find: bracelets made of human skin, four human noses in a cup on the kitchen table, a pair of human lips on a string tied to a windowsill, human skin stretched over an empty coffee can as a drum, skin from a woman's body fashioned into a vest, some belts made from human skin, a chair upholstered with human hide, the skinned faces of nine women mounted on the walls, ten heads sawed off above the eyebrows, a skull fashioned into a soup bowl, and a purse with handles made of human skin.

Bernice Worden's body was found in the summer kitchen, strung up by its heels, eviscerated and dressed out like a deer carcass. Her severed head was in a cardboard box, and her heart was found in a plastic bag on the stove.

As near as anybody could figure, there were fifteen bodies around.

Gein admitted being a murderer, cannibal, and necrophile. He was most upset about having taken a cash register and $41 from Mrs. Worden's general store. "I'm no robber. I took the money and the register only because I wanted to see how the machine worked."

Diagnosed as a chronic schizophrenic, Gein was found mentally unfit to stand trial and was never convicted of any crimes, but he spent the remainder of his life confined to institutions for the criminally insane. He died of a respiratory ailment at the Mendota Mental Health Institute on July 26, 1984. He was 77. He was later buried next to his mother, brother, and father.

For years, the farmhouse was pelted with rocks and snowballs. It became a symbol of evil, and one night it was torched and burned to the ground.

There was an English serial killer, Dennis Nilsen, with parallels to the Milwaukee case. A plain-looking, bespectacled man who lived alone and frequented gay bars, Nilsen admitted killing fifteen men, all of them strangers, all of them strangled, over a four-year period. The killer didn't want the men he brought back to this apartment to leave him. He kept dead bodies in his closets and under the floorboards, hauling them out to sit in chairs while he watched television or using them as turn-ons while he masturbated. He had sex of sorts with six of them, and he sometimes took Polaroid pictures of his work. When the corpses started to rot, he dismembered them, boiling severed heads on his stove and cutting out hearts and other organs. He flushed some of the remains down the toilet, and he was tripped up when a plumber noticed the sewer pipes clogged with human flesh.

The case of Nilsen, a civil servant and former constable who lived in London, England, was detailed in the 1984 book *Killing for Company* by Brian Masters.

Nilsen, thirty-seven at the time, was convicted of six counts of murder and two counts of attempted murder on November 4, 1983. He was sentenced to life in prison.

When he was arrested in February of 1983, police found the parts of three bodies in a clothes closet, a tea chest, and a drawer in the bathroom. He had set out deodorant sticks to mask the stench.

He said twelve murders were committed at a previous address, where he had burned some remains and buried bones in a backyard. In his statements to police he said he had tried to kill seven others, but either something had gone awry or the men got away.

In the media frenzy for details, a Japanese crew holed up in a house near the police station, and armed with sensitive listening devices, tried to eavesdrop on the revelations Nilsen was calmly giving authorities.

Nilsen, the second of three children from a broken home, had a taste for alcohol and worked as a cook in the British Army. Of his first victim in 1979, Nilsen told police he met an Irish youth in a bar and brought him back to his apartment.

Said Nilsen, "I remember thinking that because it was morning he would wake and leave me. I became extremely aroused and I could feel my heart pounding and I began to sweat."

The victim was strangled with a necktie. Nilsen said he gave the corpse a bath, which became a ritual for those who followed. He later wanted to sodomize the corpse, but couldn't stay aroused. He kept the body under some floorboards for seven months before he burned it.

Nilsen said the killings gave him a sense of power that eased his loneliness. "I remember being thrilled that I had full control and ownership of this beautiful body," he told authorities in reference to one killing.

He said each act was one of compulsion. "My

sole reason for existence was to carry out that act at that moment," Nilsen said.

He also told authorities, "I wanted a warm relationship and someone to talk to. . . . I was the forlorn seeker after a relationship which was always beyond my reach. . . . The only similarity was a need not to be alone. It was to have someone to talk to and be with . . . I probably did enjoy those acts of killing. It was intense and all-consuming. How the hell do I know what motivated me to kill someone I had nothing against at that particular time! I needed to do what I did at that time. I had no control over it then. It was a powder keg waiting for a match. I was the match. . . . The real answer might lie in the fact that I could be just a bad bastard."

13

The Rubble

The most visible symbol of the Jeffrey Dahmer case is the rectangular Oxford Apartments building where Dahmer lived for fourteen months.

A steady stream of gawkers and curiosity-seekers have flowed past the site since the grisly discoveries of July 22. People take pictures or just stand and stare. Some have ventured into an adjoining alley to collect dirt and other items as souvenirs.

Tour buses, wedding parties, and stretch limousines with tinted windows have driven past the property.

It was the backdrop for a number of news conferences by politicians, clergy, and community leaders. Countless TV reporters did their standups in front of it. Several ministers have come by to pray in front of its grassy slope and bless the structure to chase away evil. The Rev. Jesse Jackson stopped by on his visit to Milwaukee. There have been marches, vigils, and demonstrations surrounding it.

"It's been a living hell. It's like we're on a zoo tour. People drive by day and night," said John Batchelor, one of the residents. "I've got to get the hell out of here. We've all got to get the hell out of here."

The building was recently appraised at $531,000. Alderman Paul Henningsen, whose district includes Dahmer's neighborhood, has proposed to the city council that the building be bought and then torn down.

"I would say that the community consensus is that this should be taken down. We don't want it to be a source of pain," Henningsen said. "My prediction is that the building will be down by the beginning of next year, if not earlier."

He plans to ask the city for money to purchase the building, help tenants relocate, and then raze the apartments.

The Christian Civil Liberties Union has said it will seek donations to buy and destroy the place. The Rev. Thomas Ponchik compared it to the McDonald's Restaurant in San Ysidro, California.

The restaurant was torn down and replaced with a memorial to 21 people gunned down in a 1984 shoot-out.

"This building is a disgrace to Milwaukee," said Robert Braun, founder of the CCLU. "It should be razed like those Nazi concentration camps and replaced with a memorial. It's symbolic of evil. I call it the 'House of Horrors.' Tear that building to the ground. It's the devil's own workshop over there."

A community group called Avenues West Association hopes a memorial is placed at the Oxford to list victims' names.

"It would be a nice thing if that space could become a park or a small garden or something else," said Minor Vandermade of the community group.

Things got so bad the city helped residents of the Oxford Apartments beat the stress August 5. With the help of an anonymous donor and the Indian Health Board, the city treated residents to a night at a hotel so they could escape the unwanted spotlight.

"Some people just couldn't take it anymore. People deserve a night free of harassment," said Mayor John Norquist.

The mayor pleaded with the media not to disclose the name of the place where residents stayed. "The reporter that breaks this story has no soul, because these people need to have some privacy."

* * *

John Batchelor didn't have much time to think about what had happened in Apartment 213 until almost sixteen hours after police rang his buzzer. He spent that first morning banished from his apartment, and on the sidewalk outside was almost constantly standing before a TV camera or reporter's notebook. He was on local and national newscasts, and appeared live with the cast of *Milwaukee's Talking,* which preempted its regular show to broadcast from the sidewalk outside Jeff Dahmer's apartment building. Batchelor finally made it up to his unit shortly before noon, and as police cleared everything including the carpeting and drapes from across the hall, his answering machine was blinking with more interview requests from around the world.

Soon, Batchelor would be less willing to talk with eager media, after he and other residents found themselves the target of the misplaced hatred of community members desperate for something solid and real to blame for Jeff Dahmer. A city slips into a state of "frozen shock" when faced with murders so brutal, Marlene Young, executive director of the National Organization for Victim Assistance, would explain the following week. Or, as former resident Randy Jones would say a month later, "My life is in danger now. There are sick people out there and I have to remember that."

But that first evening, as Batchelor walked out

of his upstairs apartment and past Dahmer's padlocked door, scarred with a pink EVIDENCE sign,
that particular sickness was beyond him. Because
that walk past Dahmer's door was his first true
realization of the sickness within. "That's when it
started getting to me," he said. "My nerves got real
bad then. I wasn't able to sleep or eat. I started
shaking all the time. From then on it made me sick
every time I had to walk past that door to take out
my garbage."

His neighbor, Pamela Bass, would tell reporters
that her sleep that night was haunted with the image
of Jeffrey Dahmer. "With the house all dark, I was
seeing him sitting at my table," she said. "I woke
up gasping."

Batchelor's hands started shaking so badly that
he couldn't hold a cup of coffee. Randy Jones
started to break down and cry just from watching
the news. The residents of the Oxford Apartments
started sleeping together in the hallway because
they were afraid to be alone. If this all could be
explained as their way of coming to grips with the
realization of the evil that lurked behind that door
for fourteen months, if the roots of their fear could
be found even in the murky depths of Jeffrey Dahmer's own character, their story would barely warrant being told. But instead their story is about the
malice that can come only from the heart of a city

in "frozen shock" as its people searched for their own answers to Dahmer.

"We got packs of hate mail," said twenty-four-year-old Randy Jones, whose first-floor apartment became a sort of meeting ground for the panicked, nerve-wracked residents. One was written in black and red, he said, and that was explained in the letter: black was for death and red for blood. "They all said the same thing—we should have known what was going on. They all blamed us. We had shootings, we had bomb threats, we had phone calls. People were blaming us, verbally harassing us and shooting at us."

One of the bullets pierced the back door nearest Dahmer's apartment, Batchelor said. "The hole is probably still there today." Other shots were fired at the ceiling-to-floor glass windows on three sides of the building's lobby. Death threats and bomb threats, the residents felt, were ignored by police officers who took the calls—except when a supervisor was at the district, and then Jones said they usually were told not to go outside and to call back if the threats persisted.

"I got a couple of calls," Batchelor said. "One caller said they knew who I was and where I worked and they would get me—I'd better watch my back." He said the call came the same evening the apartment got two bomb threats—and police told him not to go out of the building. "I had to go to the store for cigarettes," he explained. "So I told my neighbors and they all walked to the store with me, keeping me in the middle of them so nobody could shoot me. I was scared as hell. My nerves were real bad."

It was enough, he said, to drive one of the residents crazy. He'd scream obscenities at the curiosity-seekers and once, Batchelor said, the resident took up one of the Dahmer visitors to see the door—and then beat and robbed him in the hallway. "We called police and they took him [the resident] to the hospital," he said. "But they let him out the next day. Now he just sits there yelling obscenities at the sun."

Another of the residents attacked a man who came into the building screaming, "How could you fuckers not smell the smell? Don't you fucking assholes know what a dead person smells like?" The intruder ran as soon as Batchelor pulled the neighbor from him.

The visits to 924 N. 25th Street may have started more out of curiosity than malice, but even in their more harmless forms they were difficult to bear for the victims Dahmer had left behind. That first night, police had to block the streets off through morning, because so many thousands of people wanted a glimpse of the killing place that the officers themselves couldn't make their way through the streets. When the barricades were removed the gawkers returned. "For a while every day looked like a Sunday afternoon at the state fair," said Jones, who soon became the residents' advocate, working to get protection and eventually new homes for Dahmer's former neighbors.

That first morning, the traffic and parked cars—both police and civilian—so surrounded the building that Jones couldn't get his car out of the parking lot and down the street to get to his job as a supervisor aide and track coach at an area high school. "But when I did go back to work it was even worse—the constant questions, the badgering: 'Didn't you see anything? What about that smell?' Every time I'm with more than one person now I worry that they'll double-team me and find me to blame for what happened there."

Throughout the next week, the normally quiet, seldom-traveled side street was like an expressway, said Batchelor. "We couldn't even sit outside," he said. "People would stop and look at you for a minute or two and then step on the gas and take off laughing. They would yell 'Dahmer' out the window as they drove past, at all hours of the night. That can drive you nuts. You couldn't stay in your apartment because it made you sick and you hated to be alone, but you couldn't go outside either. So we just wound up staying in the hallway."

But the thousands of people outside the building were nothing compared to the hundreds brave enough to make their way inside. "I'm the type of person—I really love my privacy," Jones said. "So I was very offended by the people running through the building, trying to see whatever they thought it was they would see. To this day there are people running through there knocking on doors."

The Dahmer story was all Milwaukee—and much of the country—was talking about, and Dahmer's sick fame also translated itself into a morbid, inexplicable outgrowth of human nature that made it something of an accomplishment to brag that you had actually seen that padlocked door.

"There were people coming from out of town and they would ask us to let them in 'just so I can just see the door,' " Batchelor said. "These were whole families coming, with little kids. They'd say 'We want to feel the door and see if we can smell the smell.' "

Sometimes busloads of people would be driven by. And sometimes Batchelor would wake up in the middle of the night to a group of ten or twelve people standing in the hallway just smelling or touching the door to Jeffrey Dahmer's former apartment. "We had to run them out," he said. "We had to yell and scream. But they didn't understand. They only wanted to smell the door."

Though guests normally need to be buzzed into the building, curiosity seekers angry that no one would let them in tore a back door off the hinges, giving them unlimited access to the building. "There were constantly strange people lurking all around. We had to yell at them, 'Hey, get the hell out of here,' but a lot of times they wouldn't listen until we went crazy," Batchelor said.

But worse, at least as far as Batchelor's nerves were concerned, were the visits from the families of some of the eleven young men whose slaughtered remains were carried out of Dahmer's apartment. "I would just be sitting outside and they would come up and say 'My son got killed here. Can you show me the apartment?' So I would take them in."

Conversation was difficult as the families made their way to the doorway. "I was really scared they would blame me and that made my nerves worse, bringing them up there and knowing that at any moment they might just jump me," Batchelor said. "But they would mostly just stand there, looking at the door, as though they thought maybe they could feel if their son was in there. Sometimes they would just look at the door or sometimes they would put their hand on it. Then they would look at me and say 'You didn't hear nothing?' I'd say no. I'd tell them, 'I'm really sorry about what happened to your family, but I didn't hear anything.' Then they'd say, 'Didn't you see anything?' And I'd have to say, 'No, I didn't see anything.' Then sometimes they would look at me like they were really angry. I

took a couple of them up there like that. I didn't
know who was who.''

Members of the homosexual community also
made the trek past Dahmer's door, Batchelor said.
''Sometimes they'd harass the women who lived
inside [the building], calling them bitches. But some
of the people who got killed in there were their
friends. Sometimes they'd be crying and others
would just be angry.''

When John Batchelor saw the fifty-seven-gallon-
barrel being taken from the building that night, he
remembered the manager telling him about the time
he told Dahmer to get that damn barrel out of his
unit. The manager had bent over the blue drum to
look inside, and said the smell almost knocked him
over.

When the story of Konerak Sinthasomphone's
near-escape came out in the press, Randy Jones
remembered a morning in late May when they
awoke to find the building's outside door slightly
smeared with blood. They assumed someone had
simply been cut on a piece of glass.

And as police released the names of seventeen
victims, one after another, the residents of 924 N.
25th Street tried to recall each person Dahmer had
entered the building with—and if they ever saw that
person leave again.

''There was one guy I used to see Dahmer with
all the time,'' Batchelor recalled. ''They'd always

be coming up the back stairs together. Then all of a sudden I didn't see him coming around anymore. At the time, I just kind of wondered about it. Now I think he must have killed him.''

There were thirty-nine residents at the Oxford Apartments on July 22. A month later, there were three. ''We are the victims people will never know about,'' Jones said. ''Our lives will never be the same.''

In his role as an advocate for the apartment residents, Jones worked first to find someone to listen, then to provide them counseling, and finally to help them move out of the Oxford Apartments. On August 1, counselors from the National Organization for Victim Assistance were in the city to hold counseling sessions in the neighborhood. ''They told us this would be with us for the rest of our lives,'' Jones recalled. ''At first I thought they were exaggerating. Now I know they were right.'' As the bomb threats, the shootings, and the harassment continued, Jones heard police deny his request for extra protection for the building, or to block off the streets as they had done when they themselves needed access. And he heard building management say there was nothing they could do to help people move or to make the conditions there safer.

''Nobody cared about what was happening to us in there,'' Jones said.

At least not in the way Jones would have hoped.

Television crews made live broadcasts from the spot for part of every newscast for over a week. TV reporters even interviewed the garbage men whose route included Dahmer's apartment.

"Every time you turned around you'd have a news reporter in front of you." Batchelor said. "It got to where I couldn't even take the trash out. I would try, and the next thing I knew the news [cameras] had gotten me. One time I didn't even have a shirt on—I was just taking out my trash. But they wanted their interview and so I said, sure, just let me get some clothes on first. They even filmed that—me walking down the hallway half-naked to get a shirt."

By August 3, the city announced that state aid was available for residents looking to move. Eventually, the city made arrangements to help the residents move. "They wanted out right now," City Commissioner of Public Works John Bolden said. And the Red Cross was authorized to provide relocation funds.

"[The residents] are obviously under a lot of stress and their minds and bodies are trying to cope with it," Jay Wallace, Red Cross director of disaster services, explained to reporters. "It's not something that's going to be resolved in the next ten or eleven days or even by moving out of the building."

Moving out of the building was, however, an exceedingly necessary first step, Jones said. "I clearly remember when we decided we had to get out of there," he said. That moment came when they saw the one-year-old son of one of the residents sitting in the hallway, rocking himself back and forth and rhythmically banging his head against the wall. "He had a huge knot on the back of his head, but wasn't even reacting in pain. Up until then we thought we had done a good job of protecting the children in the building—trying not to talk about it in front of them and all—but when we saw that we realized that the children could sense the stress that was there. And that child was acting out what all of us were feeling inside."

Of the three residents who stayed behind, two couldn't afford to move even with state assistance, and the other said he wouldn't be driven from his home of five years. "He says he's not going to let anybody force him to move out," Jones explained. "But you have sick people out there and something will happen to that building. I would have been there five years this month and I didn't want to move out myself. That was still my home. But I didn't have a choice."

Batchelor is grateful he had the chance to get out of Apartment 212. "If I had stayed there I would have ended up like that guy yelling at the sun," he said. But he said there is plenty still wrong with the former residents of the building. For instance, he said it took him a week to regain his appetite. "We still smell it in our minds. I still can't cook meat,'' he said.

At work, Batchelor said a month later he was still being told that he "was turning white." It took him over a week to return to his job, and upon his return, he said it seemed like he was constantly being confronted with Jeffrey Dahmer jokes.

"I used to be an up, happy person who joked around a lot,'' he said. "I don't like talking too much now. I guess now I'm more quiet and serious. I don't like hearing all those Dahmer jokes. When people come up to me, I'm just like, get the hell away from me.''

Regardless of how the individual residents of the Oxford Apartments responded to the nightmare, Jones said all their lives have been affected—be it how they sleep at night, respond to people at work, or watch television.

"We're trying to forget it, but we really can't,'' he said. "I can't even watch the news anymore. I find everything depressing. I can't sit there and listen about people getting shot,'' he said. The young man said he used to consider himself a tough person, "but sometimes now I just break down and cry. We're just asking for those of us who lived in that apartment to get our lives back on track. At first I thought it wouldn't affect me, but I guess I was just running from it.''

Now, Jones said, he and the other residents are

running from trust—from not knowing who to trust and not trusting anybody. And in Batchelor's new apartment, a neighbor came over to introduce herself, bringing along some homemade bread wrapped in aluminum foil. "I didn't want to hurt her feelings, so I took it from her. But I don't know that I'll eat it. I'm scared to trust. Even though she's probably a real nice lady."

And he says there are other, more physical scars from his former neighbor. "I'm still having nightmares; I'm still not sleeping real well," he said. "And just the other night, I was watching TV with a friend. It was about 2:30, and I looked around and there was this white guy looking through the screen window at me. That scared the shit out of me. I thought it was Dahmer's nephew coming to get me." Actually, Batchelor explained, it was just a drunk kid who was looking for a neighbor and came to the wrong house.

Jones said he plans on being in the courtroom for Dahmer's trial to try to answer some unanswered questions. "I need to go, just to look at him, to speak at him just in my inner self," he said.

But for former residents of the Oxford Apartments, the biggest unanswered question of all is whether they could have done anything to prevent this calamity. The question gnaws at them from within. It is a question likely to haunt them the way Jeffrey Dahmer will haunt Milwaukee.

"People say we should have known, but how many people can go home and be sure they know what their neighbor is doing every day?" Jones said.

"Jeffrey Dahmer has to be a high prince of the devil to have kept doing what he did over and over, and for it not to affect him . . ." he said without finishing the sentence. "But now you have to look at that and ask, how many more like him are out there? That neighbor you talk to over the fence every day—think about what he might be doing in his basement."

One of the three holdouts still living in the Oxford Apartments is James Hodge, forty-five, who can only recall seeing Dahmer twice in the fourteen months he was a tenant.

"He didn't appear to be someone who could do these types of things," Hodge said.

Hodge walks the empty halls of the forty-nine-unit building, mindful of the nightmares, horrors, pesky reporters, gawkers, and distractions that drove his neighbors out. He is not so stubborn as he is trapped by his own consequences.

"I'm poor. I can't afford to move," Hodge said.

He was asked if he was afraid or had nightmares like others did when the truth about the horrors behind Apartment 213 spilled out. Hodge replied without hesitation by reciting the 23rd Psalm of David: "Yea, though I walk through the valley of the shadow of death, I will fear no evil . . ."

Chronology

May 21, 1960
Jeffrey Lionel Dahmer is born in Milwaukee to the former Joyce Annette Flint and Lionel Dahmer.

June 4, 1978
Dahmer graduates from Revere High School in Bath, Ohio.

June 18, 1978
Stephen Mark Hicks of Coventry, Ohio, is last seen hitchhiking to a rock concert. Dahmer told police he brought him back to his home, then struck and strangled him with a barbell when Hicks wanted to leave. Dahmer said he disposed of the body by smashing the bones to bits with a sledgehammer.

July 24, 1978
Divorce of Joyce and Lionel Dahmer becomes final.

September, 1978
Dahmer enrolls in Ohio State University, but drops out after one semester.

December 29, 1978
Dahmer enlists in U.S. Army for three years and is later stationed in Baumholder, West Germany.

March 26, 1981
Dahmer gets early discharge because of his heavy drinking. Lives for six months in Miami, Florida.

October 7, 1981
Bath Township police charge Dahmer with disorderly conduct and resisting arrest for having an open container of alcohol.

January, 1982
Dahmer moves to West Allis, Wisconsin, to live with his grandmother.

August 8, 1982
Dahmer is charged with disorderly conduct by Wisconsin State Fair park police for lowering his pants in a crowd.

January 14, 1985
Dahmer is hired as a laborer at Ambrosia Chocolate Co.

September 8, 1986
Milwaukee Police charge Dahmer with lewd and lascivious behavior after two twelve-year-old boys

said they saw him masturbating. Charge later reduced to disorderly conduct, and Dahmer claims he
was urinating in the woods.

September 15, 1987
Steven Tuomi reported missing by his parents. Dahmer said in the fall of that year he met Tuomi at a
gay bar and went to a hotel. He said when he woke
up the man was dead, and he took the body back to
his grandmother's house to dispose of it. No remains were ever found. He said Tuomi was the first
person he killed in Wisconsin.

January 16, 1988
James Doxtator last seen by his family. Dahmer
told police he picked up Doxtator outside a gay bar,
then killed him at his grandmother's house. He said
he disposed of the body by smashing it to bits with
a sledgehammer.

March 24, 1988
Richard Guerrero is reported missing by his family.
Dahmer said he met Guerrero at a gay bar, killed
him at his grandmother's house, and disposed of the
body without a trace.

April, 1988
Ronald D. Flowers of Zion, Illinois, files complaint
with West Allis police claiming Dahmer drugged

him and stole his wallet and gold bracelet. Police investigate, but have no evidence to press charges.

September 25, 1988
Dahmer is charged with second-degree sexual assault and enticing a child for immoral purposes after luring a thirteen-year-old to his apartment at 808 N. 24th St. He promised the boy fifty dollars if he posed for pictures. Dahmer reportedly put a sleeping pill in the boy's coffee before he fondled him.

January 30, 1989
Dahmer is convicted of second-degree sexual assault and enticing a child for immoral purposes.

March 25, 1989
Dahmer said he met Anthony Sears at a gay bar, took him back to his grandmother's house, and killed him. Dahmer preserved and kept the skull. It was recovered later from his apartment in Milwaukee. He was awaiting sentencing at the time of the Sears killing.

May 23, 1989
Dahmer is sentenced to prison terms of five and three years, to be served concurrently, but Judge William Gardner stays the prison sentence. He instead confines Dahmer on a work-release arrangement and places him on five years' probation.

March 2, 1990
Dahmer is released after ten months in confinement.

May 13, 1990
Dahmer signs lease to rent No. 213 at the Oxford Apartments.

May 29, 1990
Raymond Lamont Smith is last seen by his family. Dahmer said he met Smith at a gay bar, then killed him at his apartment. Smith's skull was found there.

June 14, 1990
Edward Smith is last seen by his family. Dahmer said he met Smith at a gay bar, then killed him at his apartment. He disposed of all the remains by setting them out in bags with the trash.

September 2, 1990
Ernest Miller is last seen by his family. Dahmer said he met Miller outside a bookstore, then killed him by cutting his throat at Dahmer's apartment. Dahmer said he saved the man's skull, placed his biceps in the freezer, and preserved his skeleton.

September 24, 1990
Friends report David Thomas missing. Dahmer said he invited the man back to his apartment and killed him. He disposed of the entire body because Thomas "wasn't his type."

March 7, 1991
Curtis Straughter is last seen by his friends. Dahmer said he met the man at a bus stop near Marquette University, took him back to his apartment, and killed him. Straughter's skull was found later.

March 25, 1991
Dahmer tells his probation officer he got a phone call from his mother, the first time in five years he has heard from her.

April 7, 1991
Errol Lindsey left home to get a key made. Dahmer said he met him on the street, lured him back to his apartment, and killed him. Lindsey's skull was found in the apartment.

May 24, 1991
Anthony Hughes, a deaf-mute, disappears. Dahmer said he met Hughes at a gay bar, brought him back to the apartment, and killed him. Hughes's skull was found later.

May 26, 1991
Konerak Sinthasomphone, last seen on his way to play soccer, is lured to Dahmer's apartment. Neighborhood people say they saw the fourteen-year-old boy, naked and bleeding, wandering in the street, so they called police. Dahmer convinced police it was a homosexual lovers' quarrel and that the boy

was an adult. The boy was left in his custody. Dahmer later said the boy must have got outside while he went to buy beer. Dahmer said he killed him that night and preserved his skull.

June 30, 1991
Dahmer said he met Matt Turner after the Gay Pride parade in Chicago. They rode the bus back to Milwaukee, and Dahmer said he killed him in his apartment. Turner's head was recovered from Dahmer's freezer.

July 6, 1991
Jeremiah Weinberger is seen leaving a gay bar in Chicago with a sandy-haired white man. Dahmer said he and Weinberger took the bus back to Milwaukee, and he killed the man when he wanted to leave. Weinberger's head was found in the freezer.

July 15, 1991
Dahmer is fired from Ambrosia Chocolate Co. for chronic absenteeism.

July 15, 1991
Oliver Lacy is last seen by his family. Dahmer said he met him on the street and killed him in his apartment. Lacy's head was placed in the refrigerator; his heart and other organs in the freezer compartment.

July 19, 1991
Joseph Bradehoft disappears. Dahmer said he saw the man at a bus stop and lured him back to his apartment. Bradehoft's head was found in the freezer.

July 22, 1991
Tracy Edwards flags down a patrol car wearing handcuffs on his left wrist. He told police he escaped Dahmer's apartment after the man threatened him with a knife. Police discovered body parts when they went to check out the story.

July 25, 1991
Dahmer is charged with four counts of first-degree intentional homicide. He is held on a $1 million bond.

July 26, 1991
Three Milwaukee policemen are suspended with pay after revelations that they were at Dahmer's apartment on May 27 and allowed a fourteen-year-old Laotian boy to remain in his custody.

August 6, 1991
Prosecutors file eight more homicide charges. Bond is increased to $5 million.

August 22, 1991
Prosecutors file three homicide charges, bringing total to fifteen in Wisconsin.

Appendix: The Criminal Complaint

The following is the text of the criminal complaint the State of Wisconsin filed against Dahmer, August 21, 1991.

CIRCUIT COURT
STATE OF WISCONSIN CRIMINAL DIVISION MILWAUKEE COUNTY

STATE OF WISCONSIN, Plaintiff   **AMENDED CRIMINAL COMPLAINT**

vs.

	CRIME(S):
	See Charging Section Below
Jeffrey L. Dahmer 05/21/60	STATUTE(S) VIOLATED
924 N. 25th St.	See Charging Section Below
Milwaukee, WI	COMPLAINING WITNESS:
	Donald Domagalski
Defendant.	CASE NUMBER:
	F-912542

THE ABOVE NAMED COMPLAINING WITNESS BE-
ING DULY SWORN SAYS THAT THE ABOVE NAMED
DEFENDANT IN THE COUNTY OF MILWAUKEE,
STATE OF WISCONSIN

COUNT 01: FIRST DEGREE MURDER

in January of 1988, at 2357 South 57th Street, City of West
Allis, County of Milwaukee, did cause the death of another
human being, James E. Doxtator, with intent to kill that
person contrary to Wisconsin Statutes section 940.01.

COUNT 02: FIRST DEGREE MURDER

in March of 1988, at 2357 South 57th Street, City of West
Allis, County of Milwaukee, did cause the death of another
human being, Richard Guerrero, with intent to kill that
person contrary to Wisconsin Statutes section 940.01.

COUNT 03: FIRST DEGREE INTENTIONAL HOMICIDE

on or about March 26, 1989, at 2357 South 57th Street, City
of West Allis, County of Milwaukee, did cause the death of
another human being, Anthony Sears, with intent to kill that
person contrary to Wisconsin Statutes section 940.01(1).

COUNT 04: FIRST DEGREE INTENTIONAL HOMICIDE

during the Spring or early Summer of 1990, at 924 North
25th Street, City and County of Milwaukee, did cause the
death of another human being, Raymond Smith a/k/a Ricky
Beeks, with intent to kill that person contrary to Wisconsin
Statutes section 940.01(1).

COUNT 05: FIRST DEGREE INTENTIONAL HOMICIDE

during the Summer of 1990, at 924 North 25th Street, City
and County of Milwaukee, did cause the death of another
human being, Edward W. Smith, with intent to kill that
person contrary to Wisconsin Statutes section 940.01(1).

COUNT 06: FIRST DEGREE INTENTIONAL HOMICIDE

on or about September 3, 1990, at 924 North 25th Street,
City and County of Milwaukee, did cause the death of
another human being, Ernest Miller, with intent to kill that
person contrary to Wisconsin Statutes section 940.01(1).

COUNT 07: FIRST DEGREE INTENTIONAL HOMICIDE

on or about September 24, 1990, at 924 North 25th Street,
City and County of Milwaukee, did cause the death of
another human being, David Thomas, with intent to kill that
person contrary to Wisconsin Statutes section 940.01(1).

COUNT 08: FIRST DEGREE INTENTIONAL HOMICIDE

on or about February 18, 1991, at 924 North 25th Street,
City and County of Milwaukee, did cause the death of
another human being, Curtis Straughter, with intent to kill
that person contrary to Wisconsin Statutes section
940.01(1).

COUNT 09: FIRST DEGREE INTENTIONAL HOMICIDE

on or about April 7, 1991, at 924 North 25th Street, City and
County of Milwaukee, did cause the death of another human
being, Errol Lindsey, with intent to kill that person contrary
to Wisconsin Statutes section 940.01(1).

COUNT 10: FIRST DEGREE INTENTIONAL HOMICIDE

on or about May 24, 1991, at 924 North 25th Street, City and
County of Milwaukee, did cause the death of another human
being, Tony Anthony Hughes, with intent to kill that person
contrary to Wisconsin Statutes section 940.01(1).

COUNT 11: FIRST DEGREE INTENTIONAL HOMICIDE

on or about May 27, 1991, at 924 North 25th Street, City and
County of Milwaukee, did cause the death of another human

being, Konerak Sinthasomphone, with intent to kill that person contrary to Wisconsin Statutes section 940.01(1).

COUNT 12: FIRST DEGREE INTENTIONAL HOMICIDE

on or about June 30, 1991, at 924 North 25th Street, City and County of Milwaukee, did cause the death of another human being, Matt Turner a/k/a/ Donald Montrell, with intent to kill that person contrary to Wisconsin Statutes section 940.01(1).

COUNT 13: FIRST DEGREE INTENTIONAL HOMICIDE

on or about July 7, 1991, at 924 North 25th Street, City and County of Milwaukee, did cause the death of another human being, Jeremiah Weinberger, with intent to kill that person contrary to Wisconsin Statutes section 940.01(1).

COUNT 14: FIRST DEGREE INTENTIONAL HOMICIDE

on or about July 15, 1991 at 924 North 25th Street, City and County of Milwaukee, did cause the death of another human being, Oliver Lacy, with intent to kill that person contrary to Wisconsin Statutes section 940.01(1).

COUNT 15: FIRST DEGREE INTENTIONAL HOMICIDE

on or about July 19, 1991 at 924 North 25th Street, City and County of Milwaukee, did cause the death of another human being, Joseph Bradehoft, with intent to kill that person contrary to Wisconsin Statutes section 940.01(1).

HABITUAL CRIMINALITY

on January 30, 1989, Jeffrey L. Dahmer was convicted in the Circuit Court of Milwaukee County in Circuit Court Case Number F-882515 of the felony offenses of Second Degree Sexual Assault and Enticing a Child for Immoral Purposes in violation of 940.225(2)(e) and 944.12 of the Wisconsin Statutes, and that said convictions remain of record and unreversed and therefore defendant is a repeater pursuant to Wisconsin Statutes 939.62, and is subject to a total sentence of not more than ten (10) years on each count recited in addition to the mandatory life sentence for each count of First Degree Intentional Homicide and First Degree Murder.

Upon conviction of each count of First Degree Intentional Homicide and count of First Degree Murder, Class A Felonies, the penalty is life imprisonment.

Complainant states that he is a Captain of Police with the City of Milwaukee Police Department and bases this complaint upon the following:

VICTIM JAMES DOXTATOR, DOB: 3/1/73

1) Upon the statement of the defendant, which statement is against (the defendant's) penal interest that in January of 1988 he met a young male he thought was Hispanic who was waiting for a bus in front of the 219 Club on 2nd Street in the City and County of Milwaukee, State of Wisconsin; he (the defendant) approached him and asked him if he would like to make some money by posing in the nude, viewing videos, and having a drink at (the defendant's) residence; at this time he (the defendant) lived at South 57th Street in the City of West Allis, County of Milwaukee, State of Wisconsin; the two of them went to that location by bus and they had sex and then he gave the young male a drink with sleeping potion and after he passed out killed him by strangling him; he dismembered him and smashed bones with a sledgehammer and disposed of them; he did not keep any portion of this individual; further he remembers that the young male told him that he lived with his mother in the vicinity of 10th and National; he further recalls that the young male had two scars close to each of his (the young male's) nipples that were approximately the circumference of a cigarette; the defendant viewed a copy of a booking photo of James E. Doxtator, DOB 3/1/73, that had been taken on September 23, 1987 and indicated that he was 75% sure that this was the male that he met by the bus stop although he remembered him as looking somewhat older and heavier.

2) Upon the statement of Debra Vega, an adult citizen, that she (Vega) in January of 1988 lived at 1010 East Pierce in the City and County of Milwaukee, State of Wisconsin, and that her son is James E. Doxtator, DOB 3/1/73; she reported her son missing on January 18, 1988 and has never seen him since or been contacted by him since; further her son had two small scars in the area of his nipples that looked like cigarette burns; also that her home in 1988 at 1010 East Pierce was approximately one block from 10th and National; also that her son was a Native American.

VICTIM RICHARD GUERRERO, DOB: 12/12/65

1) Upon the further statement of the defendant, that in approximately March of 1988 he (the defendant) met a Hispanic male in the Phoenix Bar located on 2nd Street near the 219 Club in the City and County of Milwaukee, State of Wisconsin; he (the defendant) asked this man to come to his residence which at that time was his grandmother's house located at 2357 South 57th Street in the City of West Allis, County of Milwaukee, State of Wisconsin; he asked the man to come to look at videos and take photos or engage in sex and the man came with him; they had oral sex at the house and then he drugged the man; while the man was drugged he killed him and dismembered the body and disposed of it completely without keeping any parts; he recalls that he later saw in the personal section of a local newspaper a photo of this victim and a report that he was missing; further the defendant viewed a photograph from the January 7, 1989 Milwaukee Journal of Richard Guerrero, DOB: 12-12-65, and identified this as the person he killed in this incident.

2) Upon the statement of Pablo Guerrero, an adult citizen, that he (Guerrero) is the father of Richard Guerrero and that he has not seen his son since mid March, 1988; at that time he (Pablo Guerrero) reported his son as missing to the Milwaukee Police Department; further that advertisements with his son's picture were placed in local newspapers indicating that his son was missing.

VICTIM ANTHONY SEARS, D.O.B.: 1/28/65

1) Upon the further statement of the defendant, that he met Anthony Sears (whom he identified in a photograph) at

a club called La Cage; that a friend of Anthony Sears drove him (the defendant) and Anthony Sears to the area of his (the defendant's) grandmother's house in the City of West Allis, County of Milwaukee, State of Wisconsin; that his grandmother's house is 2357 South 57th Street; that after they arrived at that residence they had sex and he gave Anthony Sears a drink with sleeping pills in it and that he strangled him and dismembered the body; that he kept Anthony Sears' head and boiled it to remove the skin; further, that he kept the skull and painted it.

2 Upon the statement of Jeffrey Connor, an adult citizen, that he (Connor) was with Anthony Sears on the evening of March 25th, 1989 and on that evening they were at a bar on 6th and National; they closed the bar and that Anthony Sears had met a white male named Jeff who said that he was here from Chicago and was visiting his grandmother who lived at 56th and Lincoln; that he (Connor) than gave Jeff and Anthony Sears a ride to the vicinity of 56th and Lincoln where they (Jeff and Sears) got out of the car and walked southbound.

3) Upon complainant's personal knowledge of addresses in Milwaukee County and that the intersection of 56th and Lincoln is north of and in close proximity to the address 2357 South 57th Street in the City of West Allis.

4) Upon the statement of Dr. Jeffrey Jentzen, Milwaukee County Medical Examiner, that during the early morning hours of July 23rd, 1991 he (Jentzen) with Milwaukee police officers and other members of the County of Milwaukee Medical Examiner's Office was present at 924 North 25th Street in the City and County of Milwaukee, State of Wisconsin in Apartment 213; that he was present at that location when seven human skulls (three of which were painted), four human heads, and numerous other body parts were recovered; that all the human remains were transported to the Milwaukee County Medical Examiner's Office.

5) Upon the statement of Dr. L. T. Johnson, a Forensic Odontologist, that he (Johnson) made a comparison of the painted human skulls recovered from 924 North 25th Street in the City and County of Milwaukee, State of Wisconsin during the early morning hours of July 23rd, 1991 with

known dental records of Anthony Sears and determined that one of the painted skulls is that of Anthony Sears.

VICTIM RAYMOND SMITH A/K/A RICKY BEEKS, D.O.B.: 8/10/57

1) Upon the further statement of the defendant that approximately two months after he (the defendant) moved into Apartment 213 at 924 North 25th Street in the City and County of Milwaukee, State of Wisconsin he met a black male at the 219 Club and offered him money to be photographed and have a drink and watch videos; that the man agreed and came with him (the defendant) to 924 North 25th Street, Apartment 213; that at that location he (the defendant) gave the man a drink which was drugged and the man fell asleep; that he (the defendant) then strangled the man and removed the man's clothing and had oral sex with him; further, that he dismembered the body but kept the skull and later painted it; further, that he (the defendant) identified photographs of Raymond Lamont Smith as being the photographs of the man to whom he had done this.

2) Upon the further statement of Dr. L. T. Johnson that he (Johnson) examined the painted skulls recovered at 924 North 25th Street in the City and County of Milwaukee, State of Wisconsin during the early morning hours of July 23rd, 1991 with known dental records of Raymond Lamont Smith and determined that one of the aforementioned skulls is that of Raymond Smith.

3) Upon your complainant's personal observation of a copy of the defendant's rental application for the living premises at 924 North 25th Street, Apartment 213; that the aforementioned rental agreement has an initial lease date of May 13th, 1990.

VICTIM EDWARD SMITH, D.O.B.: 8/2/62

1) Upon the further statement of the defendant, that during the summer of 1990, approximately in July, he met a person whom he identified through a photograph as Edward W. Smith, DOB: 8-2-62, at the Phoenix Bar on 2nd Street in

Milwaukee and offered him money for sex and to pose for pictures, they took a cab to his (the defendant's) apartment at 924 North 25th Street, in the City and County of Milwaukee, State of Wisconsin; they had oral sex and he gave Smith a drink which contained sleeping pills and then strangled him; he dismembered Smith and took four or five photos of him; he completely disposed of Edward Smith's body by placing it in garbage bags and at a later time he also got rid of the photos of Edward Smith; he further recalls that Smith wore a headband like an Arab.

2) Upon the statement of Carolyn Smith, an adult citizen, that she (Carolyn Smith) is the sister of Edward W. Smith and that she has had no contact with him since June 23, 1990; further that her brother was called "the Sheik" because he frequently wore a turban-like wrap on his head.

VICTIM ERNEST MILLER, D.O.B.: 5/5/67

1) Upon the statement of Vivian Miller, an adult citizen, that she (Miller) is the aunt of Ernest Miller and that on September 1st, 1990 Ernest Miller came from his home in Chicago to Milwaukee to visit for the Labor Day weekend and that he left her home during the early morning hour of September 3rd, 1990 and she has not seen him or heard from him since.

2) Upon the further statement of the defendant that during the summer of 1990 he met a black male (whom he identified through a photograph of Ernest Miller as being Ernest Miller) in front of a book store in the 800 block of North 27th Street in the City and County of Milwaukee, State of Wisconsin and that he offered the man money to return to his (the defendant's) apartment at 924 North 25th Street in the City and County of Milwaukee, State of Wisconsin; that when they returned to his apartment they had sex and then he (the defendant) drugged Ernest Miller and killed him by cutting his throat; further, that after taking photos of him, he dismembered the body and disposed of the flesh except for the biceps which he kept in the freezer; he also kept the skull which he painted after the skin was removed, and he kept the skeleton which he bleached.

3) Upon the further statement of Dr. L. T. Johnson that he (Johnson) has compared the painted skulls recovered on July 23rd, 1991 from the defendant's apartment at 924 North 25th Street in the City and County of Milwaukee, State of Wisconsin with known dental records of Ernest Miller and determined that one of the aforementioned painted skulls is that of Ernest Miller.

VICTIM DAVID C. THOMAS, D.O.B.: 12/21/67

1) Upon the further statement of the defendant that he in the autumn of 1990 met a black male in the vicinity of 2nd and Wisconsin in the City and County of Milwaukee, State of Wisconsin and offered the man money to come to his apartment at 924 North 25th Street; when they got to his apartment they drank and talked but he had no sex with this man because the man wasn't his type; that he gave the man a drink with a sleeping potion in it and killed him even though he did not want to have sex with him because he thought the man would wake up and be angry; that he dismembered the body but did not keep any of the body parts because the man wasn't his type; further, that he photographed the man while he was in the process of dismembering him.

2) Upon the statement of Chandra Beanland, an adult citizen, that she (Beanland) is the girlfriend of David C. Thomas and that she reported him missing on September 24th, 1990 to the Milwaukee Police Department.

3) Upon the statement of Brian O'Keefe, a City of Milwaukee Police Detective, that he (O'Keefe) contacted the family of David C. Thomas in the course of this investigation and specifically spoke with Leslie Thomas who identified herself as David C. Thomas' sister and that he (O'Keefe) showed Leslie Thomas the facial portion of the photograph which the defendant identified as having been taken during the course of dismembering David Thomas; further, that the facial portion showed no injuries at the time it was shown to Leslie Thomas and that Leslie Thomas identified the person in the photograph as being her brother, David Thomas; that the Thomas family supplied a photograph of David Thomas

sleeping which they had; further that the face in this family photograph appeared to him (O'Keefe) to depict the same individual as in the photograph the defendant had taken while dismembering this victim.

VICTIM CURTIS STRAUGHTER, D.O.B.: 4/16/73

1) Upon the statement of Katherine Straughter, an adult citizen, that she (Straughter) is the grandmother of Curtis Straughter and that she last saw her grandson on February 18th, 1991.

2) Upon the further statement of the defendant that in February of 1991 he observed Curtis Straughter (whom he identified through a photograph) waiting for a bus by Marquette University and offered him money to come back to his apartment at 924 North 25th Street in the City and County of Milwaukee, State of Wisconsin; that Straughter did accompany him back and at the apartment he (the defendant) gave Curtis Straughter a drugged drink and had oral sex with him; the defendant then strangled him with a strap and dismembered the body; he also took photos and kept the man's skull.

3) Upon the further statement of Dr. L. T. Johnson that he (Johnson) compared the unpainted skulls recovered from the defendant's apartment with known dental records of Curtis Straughter and determined that one of the unpainted skulls was that of Curtis Straughter.

VICTIM ERROL LINDSEY, D.O.B.: 3/3/72

1) Upon the statement of Yahuna Barkley, an adult citizen, that she (Barkley) is the sister of Errol Lindsey and that she last saw him on April 7th, 1991 when he went to the store and that she has not seen him since that time.

2) Upon the further statement of the defendant that in the Spring of 1991 he met Errol Lindsey (whom he identified by photograph) on the corner of 27th and Kilbourn in the City and County of Milwaukee, State of Wisconsin and that he offered Errol Lindsey money to return with him (the defendant) to his apartment at 924 North 25th Street in the

City and County of Milwaukee, State of Wisconsin; that after they returned to his apartment he gave Lindsey a drugged drink and after he fell asleep he strangled Lindsey and then had oral sex with him; he then dismembered the body and saved the skull.

3) Upon the further statement of Dr. L. T. Johnson that he (Johnson) compared the unpainted skulls recovered from the defendant's apartment on July 23rd, 1991 with known dental records of Errol Lindsey and determined that one of the unpainted skulls is that of Errol Lindsey.

VICTIM TONY ANTHONY HUGHES, D.O.B.: 8/26/59

1) Upon the further statement of the defendant that in May of 1991 he met Tony Anthony Hughes (whom he identified through a photograph) who was deaf and mute in front of the 219 Bar on Second Street in the City and County of Milwaukee, State of Wisconsin; that he communicated with Hughes by writing and it appeared that Hughes could read lips; that he offered Hughes $50 to come to his (the defendant's) apartment at 924 North 25th Street in the City and County of Milwaukee, State of Wisconsin to take photos and view videos; further, that he gave Hughes a drink with a sleeping potion and then killed him and dismembered his body and kept his skull.

2) Upon the further statement of Dr. L. T. Johnson that he (Johnson) has compared the unpainted skulls found in the apartment of the defendant with known dental records of Tony Hughes and determined that one of the unpainted skulls is that of Tony Hughes.

3) Upon the statement of Shirley Hughes, an adult citizen, that she (Hughes) is the mother of Tony Hughes and that Tony Hughes came to Milwaukee from Madison during the late afternoon or evening of May 24th, 1991 and that she has not seen him since and further that her son, Tony Hughes, is deaf and mute.

VICTIM KONERAK SINTHASOMPHONE, D.O.B.: 12/2/76

1) Upon the statement of Sounthone Sinthasomphone, an adult resident that he is the father of Konerak Sinthasom-

phone who was 14 years of age and that during the afternoon of May 26th, 1991 his son left home and did not return and he has not seen him since.

2) Upon the further statement of the defendant that he (the defendant) in late May of 1991 met a young Oriental male (whom he identified by photograph as Konerak Sintha-somphone) in front of Grand Avenue Mall in Milwaukee and that they went back to his (the defendant's) apartment at 924 North 25th Street in the City and County of Milwaukee, State of Wisconsin; that Sinthasomphone posed for two photographs while he was alive and that he (the defendant) gave Sinthasomphone a drink laced with a sleeping potion, and that they then watched videos and while they were watching videos, Sinthasomphone passed out; that he (the defendant) then had oral sex with Sinthasomphone and then he (the defendant) went to a bar to get some beer because he had run out; that while he was walking back from the bar located on 27th just north of Kilbourn, he saw Sinthasom-phone staggering down the street and he (the defendant) went up to Sinthasomphone and then the police stopped him; that he told the police that he was a friend of this individual and that the individual had gotten drunk and done this before; that the police escorted them back to his (the defendant's) apartment and he told the police he would take care of Sinthasomphone because he was his friend; that they went into the apartment and after the police left, he killed Sinthasomphone by strangling him and then had oral sex with him and then he took more photographs and dismem-bered the body and kept the skull.

3) Upon the further statement of Dr. L. T. Johnson that he (Johnson) compared the unpainted skulls recovered from the apartment at 924 North 25th Street with known dental records of Konerak Sinthasomphone and determined that one of the skulls which was recovered from that location that of Konerak Sinthasomphone.

VICTIM MATT TURNER A/K/A DONALD MONTRELL, D.O.B.: 7/3/70

1) Upon the further statement of the defendant that on June 30th, 1991 after the Gay Pride Parade in Chicago, he

met a black male at the Chicago Bus Station and offered him money to pose nude and also view videos at his apartment back in Milwaukee; he (the defendant), with this black male, returned to Milwaukee on a Greyhound Bus and then took a City Vet cab to his (the defendant's) residence in Apartment 213 at 924 North 25th Street in the City and County of Milwaukee, State of Wisconsin; he (the defendant) gave the black male something to drink which had been drugged and the man passed out and he (the defendant) used a strap to strangle the man and then dismembered him and kept his head and put it in the freezer in his apartment and placed his body in a 57 gallon barrel that he had in his residence; further that he (the defendant) looked at a photograph supplied by the Chicago Police Department of Matt Turner a/k/a Donald Montrell and indicated that he thought this was the person that he had killed in this incident.

VICTIM JEREMIAH WEINBERGER, D.O.B.: 9/29/67

1) Upon the further statement of the defendant that on or about July 5th, 1991 he met a Puerto Rican male at Carol's Gay Bar on Wells Street in Chicago and that he offered the man money to come with him to Milwaukee to pose for him and to view videos; they took a Greyhound Bus from Chicago to Milwaukee and then took a cab to the defendant's apartment at 924 North 25th Street in the City and County of Milwaukee, State of Wisconsin; this man stayed with him for two days and on the first day they had oral sex and on the second day the man indicated that he wanted to leave and he (the defendant) didn't want the man to leave so he gave him a drink with a sleeping potion in it and strangled him manually and then took photos of him and dismembered the body; he then took more photos and kept the man's head in the freezer and body in the 57 gallon drum; he (the defendant) looked at a photo supplied by the Chicago Police Department of Jeremiah Weinberger and indicated that this was the man that he had killed in this incident.

2) Upon the statement of Dr. L. T. Johnson that he (Johnson) at the Milwaukee County Medical Examiner's Office compared one of the human heads recovered from the

freezer at 924 North 25th Street with known dental records of Jeremiah Weinberger and determined that the severed human head that he examined in comparison with those records was the head of Jeremiah Weinberger.

VICTIM OLIVER LACY, D.O.B.: 6/23/67

1) Upon the further statement of the defendant that on or about July 15th, 1991 he met a black male on 27th Street between State and Kilbourn in Milwaukee and that the man stated he was going to his cousin's house; he invited the man to his residence to pose for photos and the man agreed to come and model; when they got to the residence at 924 North 25th Street in the City and County of Milwaukee, State of Wisconsin, they removed their clothes and did body rubs and he gave the man a drink which had sleeping potion in it; when the man fell asleep, he strangled him and then had anal sex with him after death; he dismembered the body and placed the man's head in the bottom of the refrigerator in a box and kept the man's heart in the freezer to eat later; he also kept the man's body in the freezer; he kept the man's identification which identified the man as Oliver Lacy, date of birth 6/23/67.

VICTIM JOSEPH BRADEHOFT, D.O.B.: 1/24/66

1) Upon the further statement of the defendant that on or about July 19th, 1991 he met a white male on Wisconsin Avenue near Marquette University; the man was waiting for a bus and had a six pack under his arm; he (the defendant) got off a bus at that location and approached the man and offered him money to pose and view videos and the man agreed; they returned to the defendant's residence at 924 North 25th Street in the City and County of Milwaukee, State of Wisconsin; they had oral sex and then gave the man a drink with a sleeping potion in it and then strangled him with a strap while he slept; he dismembered this man and put his head in the freezer and his body in the same blue 57 gallon barrel where he had placed the bodies of the black male and the Puerto Rican male; he kept this man's identifi-

cation card which identified him as Joseph Bradehoft, date
of birth 1/24/66.

AS TO VICTIMS TURNER, LACY AND BRADEHOFT

1) Upon the statement of Dr. Jeffrey Jentzen, Medical
Examiner for Milwaukee County, that on July 23rd, 1991 he
was called by the Milwaukee Police Department to Apartment 213 at 924 North 25th Street in the City and County of
Milwaukee, State of Wisconsin and inside the apartment at
that location, among other evidence, he observed a refrigerator with a freezer section; the refrigerator contained a
human head and the freezer section contained human body
parts; also there was a floor standing freezer which was
found to contain three human heads and other body parts
and there was a 57 gallon drum which contained human body
parts. Jentzen further stated that at the Milwaukee County
Medical Examiner's Office these human body parts were
examined and that fingerprints were lifted from hands that
had been found at the scene and also efforts at dental
identification were made; that Dr. L. T. Johnson, whom he
(Jentzen) knows to be a forensic odontologist, did the dental
examination and that fingerprint lifts were submitted to the
Milwaukee Police Department Bureau of Identification for
analysis.

2) Upon the statement of Wayne Peterson, that he (Peterson) is a Bureau of Identification technician and supervisor
employed by the City of Milwaukee Police Department and
that he (Peterson) made comparisons of fingerprints lifted by
the Milwaukee County Medical Examiner's Office from
body parts recovered at 924 North 25th Street on July 23rd,
1991 with known prints of various persons and was able to
identify the prints of Oliver Lacy, Joseph Bradehoft, and
Matt Turner a/k/a Donald Montrell as having been lifted from
human body parts discovered in that apartment.

AS TO HABITUAL CRIMINALITY

Complainant further states that he has viewed a certified
copy of Judgment of Conviction in Milwaukee County Cir-

cuit Court Case No. F-882515 and a copy of that Judgment of Conviction is attached hereto and incorporated herein and the aforementioned Judgment of Conviction indicated that the defendant was convicted of felony offenses in Milwaukee County within five years of the offenses listed in this complaint and that he (the defendant) is therefore a Habitual Criminal.